SUCCESSFUL GARDENING

PLANT
PARTNERS

Published by The Reader's Digest Association Limited.

First Edition Copyright © 1994
The Reader's Digest Association Limited,
Berkeley Square House, Berkeley Square, London W1X 6AB

Copyright © 1994

The Reader's Digest Association Far East Limited
Philippines Copyright 1994
The Reader's Digest Association Far East Limited

Reprinted 1995

Consultant editor: Lizzie Boyd

Typeset by SX Composing Limited in Century Schoolbook

PRINTED IN SPAIN

ISBN 0 276 42092 6

Opposite: A long-lasting partnership consisting of tall *Euphorbia characias wulfenii*
above clumps of bright yellow *E. polychroma* and daisy-flowered *Argyranthemum*
'Jamaica Primrose' achieves flower harmony and pleasing foliage contrast.

Overleaf: Backed by climbers and wall shrubs, a summer medley of pinks and blues
including lilies, roses, lavenders and phlox, grow in happy companionship. They are
tempered by white petunias and fronted by bedding plants and ground-hugging
alpines.

PUBLISHED BY THE READER'S DIGEST ASSOCIATION LIMITED
LONDON NEW YORK MONTREAL SYDNEY CAPE TOWN

Originally published in partwork form
by Eaglemoss Publications Limited

SUCCESSFUL GARDENING

PLANT
PARTNERS

Plant partners

Few plants grow in isolation either in their natural environment or in the garden. They are usually surrounded by others that thrive in the same conditions and produce haphazard though often spectacular associations. When arranging plant groupings in a garden, their requirements in terms of soil, light and water are as important as their size, shape and colour.

After this, imagination and a knowledge of a plant's performance determine whether a garden remains 'ordinary' or becomes an inspiring series of 'plant pictures'. Choosing plants is always personal and subjective, so the illustrations of plant partners in this book are intended to offer suggestions and, hopefully, inspiration for experimenting with colour and form. Some plants are so outstanding that they deserve to be seen in solitary splendour, but the majority are enhanced by the company of others.

CONTENTS

Tree partners White willow, sycamore and Japanese maple guard conifers, shrubs and colourful perennials.

Tree options

There are many reasons for choosing and planting garden trees – no other plants have as much visual impact, and trees define a garden's structure and content. They can add height to a flat landscape and help to obscure eyesores. They also introduce sound and movement within the garden and filter winds and external noises.

Numerous garden trees are available, and selection must ultimately depend on the size and shape of the plot. Always bear in mind the eventual height and spread of a mature tree – the beautiful snowdrop tree (*Halesia*) may be purchased as a slender sapling, but after 20 years it will have grown to a height of 12m (40ft), with an even wider spread. However, there are trees for every garden, ranging from narrow columns to round-headed varieties, from low and spreading Japanese maples for small gardens to weeping willows that cast shade on warm summer days. Additionally, you can choose between deciduous trees and evergreens, solemn conifers and airy gum trees. Leaves come in every shade of green through to golden, grey, purple and variegated types.

Beauty is evident throughout the year – the elegant tracery and gleaming white trunks of birches in winter, the swelling of buds and the unfolding of fresh young leaves in spring, the summer blossom of Japanese cherries and of crab apples, and the glorious autumn colours and clustered berries of rowans and whitebeams. Golden yews, blue spruces and sculptural hollies add their calming presence all year round.

In large gardens, trees planted in groups have the greatest visual impact. In smaller gardens, one well-chosen specimen tree becomes an instant focal point, especially when it is partnered by low-growing shrubs, ornamental grasses and perennials or underplanted with spring-flowering bulbs and bedding annuals.

Living trees An old fruit tree supporting a clematis spreads dappled shade over spring bulbs and foliage perennials.

TREE TEAM-UP

Give your trees impact with striking partners and clever underplanting; or group them for an impressive show.

Deciduous trees grown for the beauty of their leaves, flowers or fruit are often partnered with early flowers – particularly bulbs – before the trees are in full leaf. Alternatively, they can be under-planted with shade-tolerant, ground-covering perennials and shrubs, or partnered with ever-green trees of contrasting shape and foliage.

For example, the arching Mount Etna broom (*Genista aetnensis*), with its scented yellow pea flowers in mid summer, blends hand-somely with the pillar-like false cypress and is airy enough for summer annuals to flower beneath it.

Trees with brilliant autumn tints can create stunning pictures. For rich colour contrast, plant a paper birch (*Betula papyrifera*), with its yellow leaves and peeling white bark, next to a Japanese maple (*Acer palmatum* 'Osaka-zuki') with crimson leaves.

In winter, the white or pink flowers of the autumn- to winter-flowering cherry *Prunus subhirtella* 'Autumnalis' look even love-lier set against dark yews. Or, sur-round a pencil-thin *Juniperus scopulorum* 'Skyrocket' with winter-blooming heaths, perhaps with a conspicuously white-barked eucalyptus or a red-barked *Prunus maackii* placed behind the group.

▲ **Spring companions** Almond blossom (*Prunus dulcis*), borne on leafless branches, weaves clouds of soft pink above early daffodils.

▼ **Summer canopy** The deciduous conifer, dawn redwood (*Metasequoia glyptostroboides*), casts dappled shade over a summer underplanting of scarlet salvias and French marigolds growing between hummocks of perennial blue grass (*Festuca glauca*).

▲ **Specimen planting** The Chinese whitebeam (*Sorbus hupehensis*) is an outstanding garden tree. It unfolds its sea-green, ferny leaves in spring and its branches are decorated with clusters of white flowers in early summer. By autumn, the foliage turns yellow and red, forming a vivid contrast to the drooping bunches of red-stalked, white berries.

Such beauty is enhanced with an underplanting of *Berberis × rubrostilla* whose arching branches are studded with coral-red berries in autumn. Dwarf rhododendrons nestle below, surrounded by a glossy green carpet of *Cotoneaster dammeri* providing year-round cover.

► **Woodland associates** The moist, shady soil beneath mature trees is a favoured habitat for many types of ferns, including buckler ferns (*Dryopteris*), common polypody and the ultra-hardy shield ferns (*Polystichum*). Common ivy trails among the ferns, and dog violets (*Viola riviniana*) spread leafy ground-cover, adorned in spring with pale violet blooms.

◄ Sea of blue The Spanish bluebell (*Scilla canparulata*) is a larger plant than its English counterpart and thrives in light shade. Its spikes of clear blue bells make charming partners for the white, purple-stained goblets of *Magnolia × soulangiana* which open at the same time as the poet's narcissus 'Actaea', in late spring.

▼ Leaf contrast The autumn colours of a Japanese maple (*Acer palmatum* 'Aka Shigitatsu') change from light green and red-tinted to fiery crimson and purple. A neighbouring holly bush, the gold and green variegated *Ilex aquifolium* 'Madame Briot', lends superb contrast in colour and leaf form.

▲ Bog lovers The swamp cypress (*Taxodium distichum*) thrives in moist, boggy soil. It is clothed from late spring in bright green, frond-like foliage that turns yellow and then bronze-red before falling in autumn. The happy companions in this large bed include astilbes with their fluffy, pale pink flower plumes and the large-leaved perennial *Rodgersia podophylla*, with its chestnut-like foliage.

▲ All things bright and beautiful A glorious profusion of spring colours carpet the ground beneath the bare branches of a sycamore tree. Tall drumstick primroses (*Primula denticulata*), trumpet daffodils and chequered bells of *Fritillaria meleagris* are particularly prominent among the array. Lungwort (*Pulmonaria saccharata*) with its white-spotted leaves, spires of grape hyacinths (*Muscari*) and starry *Anemone blandas* display varied shades of blue. Clumps of low-growing *Primula vulgaris* add splashes of yellow and pale green to the spring scene.

▲ In a Japanese garden A feeling of privacy and quiet contemplation is achieved with a congenial planting of Japanese maples, bamboos and grasses. Strong variations in colour and form are evident, from the filigree maple leaves of pale green and light purple through to the dark green, linear foliage topping the canes of *Arundinaria humilis*. The grassy hummocks of golden *Hakonechloa macra* 'Aureola', planted in the foreground, add extra contrast to the scene.

► Showers of gold The easy-grown *Laburnum* × *watereri* 'Vossii' is especially spectacular in early summer. It is remarkably free-flowering — its drooping trusses of golden flowers grow as long as 60cm (2ft). Here, they rain down over a naturalized group of ornamental onions (*Allium giganteum*), softening their vivid rose-lilac flower globes.

Grouping trees

A few trees are particularly out-standing and are often best planted in isolation as individual specimens, so that nothing mars their beauty. The majority of gar-den trees, however, create a greater visual impact when they are planted in groups. Three silver birches, for example, look more attractive set in a group than when they are planted as lone trees. One variegated holly among other plain, dark green ones will lift the whole composition.

Group planting is not limited to trees of the same kind. Provided they have the same soil and site requirements, evergreen trees mix well with deciduous varieties and maintain interest when their partners have lost their leaves.

In the winter garden, weeping trees make excellent partners for evergreens, the airy grace of their leafless branches bringing a touch of lightness to the sombre greens.

The ultimate spring-time sight is a group of fruit trees in blossom. Rather than planting several of the same species together, try combining ornamental cherries and flowering crab apples to create a harmonious haze of pinks and whites. As a result, the flowering season would also be extended.

In summer, when the leaves of deciduous trees have completely unfurled, foliage colour becomes an important consideration. Use a purple-leaved tree (*Acer plata-noides* 'Crimson King' or *Prunus cerasifera* 'Nigra') or a golden-leaved one (*Gleditsia triacanthos* 'Sunburst') to add interest to a pre-dominantly green canopy. Be wary of too much purple foliage, though – it can have a dull, heavy effect.

It's worth remembering with autumn displays that not all trees colour dramatically. And those which do may assume a variety of colours which clash in a kaleido-scope of conflicting shades. Poplars and birches turn yellow, for example, while *Sorbus* trans-forms into orange and red.

In a small garden, there might be room for only one tree. Under-plant it with shrubs, perennials and bulbs that reflect or contrast with the colour of the tree foliage to create a more complete picture.

▲ **Contrasting shapes** The waterfall effect of a weeping willow (*Salix caprea* 'Kilmarnock') is emphasized by a variegated holly clipped into a formal pyramid shape. In front, the rounded form of a low-growing *Skimmia japonica* unites the group.

▼ **Springtime display** *Magnolia × soulangiana*, with its large, white goblet-shaped flowers, and *Amelanchier lamarckii*, frothing with small, white blossom, lend each other mutual support and splendour.

► **Cool corner** The magnificent golden leaves of an Indian bean tree (*Catalpa bignonioides* 'Aurea') appear almost translucent above an underplanting of yellow-flowered perennials — low-growing *Sedum reflexum* and silver-leaved *Senecio bicolor*. A nearby *Hydrangea quercifolia* adds a touch of white to the composition, though in autumn it will be transformed into a blaze of vivid foliage colours.

▼ **Sculptural forms** Two conifers create an impressive focal point in a large garden. The blue-white foliage and distinctive conical shape of *Picea pungens glauca* 'Hoopsii' are thrown into sharp relief against the bright green of *Chamaecyparis lawsoniana* 'Erecta Viridis'. The conifers rise like splendid spires from a footing of feathery ferns.

▲ **Foliage contrast** The gold-green foliage of *Robinia pseudoacacia* 'Frisia' is in airy contrast to the dense column of blue-grey *Cupressus glabra* 'Pyramidalis'.

▼ **Recalcitrant winter sweet** Patience is needed with winter sweet (*Chimonanthus praecox*): it needs both sun and shelter and usually takes seven years before it puts on its first show of winter blossom, and even then a severe frost can completely destroy it. However, in a good year, this deciduous shrub will live up to its name and wreathe the naked branches with curious claw-shaped, twisted flowers of pale lime-yellow, exquisitely scented with honey.

Winter sweet will reach a height and spread of about 2.4m (8ft) in good soil (including chalk). In winter, its rather ungainly base can be successfully hidden by the evergreen foliage and plump flowers buds of *Helleborus foetidus* and with clumps of snowdrops.

▲ **Red-barked dogwood** Annual hard pruning in spring ensures that the stems of *Cornus alba* 'Sibirica' are a bright coral-red in winter. Equally good in sun and light shade, the shrub's vivid colour can be tempered with clumps of *Crocus vernus* in delicate shades of white and pale purple.

▲ **Paper-bark maple** One of the attractions of the Chinese paper-bark maple (*Acer griseum*) is the cinnamon-coloured bark that peels off in large flakes to reveal the fresh, glowing copper colour underneath. The chestnut-like foliage of *Rodgersia podophylla* echoes the distinctive colour theme.

▲ **Pussy willow** The weeping branches of *Salix caprea* 'Kilmarnock' rain silvery catkins over an underplanting of wine-purple *Primula* × *juliana* 'Wanda'. Clumps of old-fashioned pheasant's eye (*Narcissus poeticus*), naturalized in the grassy glade, soften the vivid primrose colour.

◄ **Spring trumpeters** The graceful, weeping silver birch (*Betula pendula* 'Youngi') is ideal for the smaller garden. Its ornamental bark and curtain of green leaves which turn butter-yellow in autumn can be truly appreciated as a lawn specimen tree. In spring, its natural companions are trumpet daffodils such as 'Golden Harvest'. Winter-flowering heathers will highlight the silvery bark.

CONIFER COMPANIONS

With their beautiful form and colouring, conifers make attractive specimen trees which add charm to a variety of garden plantings.

Conifers may lack the showy blooms of flowering shrubs and trees, but they more than make up for this with their rich assortment of sizes, shapes, foliage textures and colours. They are fully hardy and easy to grow in a variety of soils. They are excellent for hedging, and yews in particular lend themselves superbly to topiary. Additionally, with a few exceptions, all conifers are evergreen.

Conifers can be an important part of garden design. They bring a bleak winter garden to life, and in summer they act as a calming backdrop to vibrant flower displays. As background trees they provide shelter and privacy.

You can create stunning effects by mixing conifers with different coloured foliage – try a tapestry hedge of green and golden false cypresses – or plant them among broadleaved trees and shrubs.

Many conifers are impressive in stature and make ideal specimen trees in large lawns and landscape designs. Conical and upright types are the most appropriate for the average garden, in groups of their own or as focal points among ornamental plants. They add height and contrasting textures when planted in heather beds. Dwarf conifers are invaluable in the rock garden, and true miniatures will thrive in sink gardens and window boxes.

Conifers are useful as focal points and foliage foils in shrub and mixed borders. The choice extends from the emerald green of *Thuja occidentalis* to the golden leaf sprays of *Chamaecyparis lawsoniana*, from the shrubby forms of the silver firs (*Abies* sp.) to the horizontal tiers of several junipers and the startling blue of the spruces (*Picea pungens glauca*).

▲ **Winter cheer** A pair of Lawson cypresses (*Chamaecyparis lawsoniana* 'Kilmacurragh') stand tall and columnar above a carpet of pink *Erica carnea* 'Winter Beauty'. The dark green foliage responds well to clipping.

▼ **Mixed border** Dwarf forms of *Chamaecyparis lawsoniana* share the same columnar lines. They span a variety of foliage colours – green, blue, grey, yellow and variegated – and are slow-growing enough to stand as feature points in herbaceous and mixed shrub borders.

◄ **Shape contrasts** The slender *Juniperus scopulorum* 'Skyrocket' needs little space and is ideal for small gardens. Its pencil-slim form contrasts splendidly with the rounded shapes of evergreen, glossy-leaved and white-flowered Mexican orange blossom (*Choisya ternata*) and pink-flowered *Daphne × burkwoodii* — both scented and in full bloom during late spring.

▼ **Golden accent** The Chinese arbor-vitae (*Thuja orientalis*) has a typical formal habit — its foliage is held in dense vertical sprays. The variety 'Semperaurea' is golden-yellow and glows throughout summer in the company of *Convolvulus althaeoides*, a sprawling mass of grey-green leaves and satiny-pink, funnel-shaped flowers. In autumn, the conifer foliage develops bronze tints.

◄ **Gold companions** The Leyland cypress (× *Cupressocyparis leylandii*) is the fastest-growing of all conifers. It is tolerant of exposure and pollution and suitable for all types of soil. It is also excellent for tall hedges and for windscreens, although in this capacity it is less suitable for small gardens.

The variety 'Castlewellan Gold' is slower-growing and with its golden-yellow foliage makes a splendid partner for a variegated dogwood (*Cornus alba* 'Spaethii').

► **Conifer groups** A mixed planting of conifers, including blue spruces, golden pines, false cypresses and tiered junipers, are partnered by a carpet of heathers and provide a colourful association for year-round interest. In autumn, the diverse shapes and colours are illuminated by the rich purple-red tints of *Amelanchier canadensis*.

▼ **Miniature conifers** Slow-growing and rarely exceeding 60cm (2ft) in height, *Juniperus communis* 'Compressa' is ideal for rock gardens, troughs and pots. Its slim upright branches are compressed into a tight columnar form, adding height to an alpine landscape. Here, two grey-green columns give substance to a grouping of golden *Potentilla tabernaemontani*, blue *Aquilegia bertolonii* and white-variegated *Arabis ferdinandi-coburgi* 'Variegata'.

◄ **Backdrop colour** The rich green, geometric outline of aromatic *Thuja orientalis* forms a perfect background for the large, clear pink blooms of the Gallica rose 'Complicata'. On warm summer days, the delicate scent from the roses blends with that of lavender at the foot of the group.

► **Mountain pines** The dwarf Siberian pine (*Pinus pumila*) is ultra-hardy and ideal for a rock or heather garden. Here, the variety 'Dwarf Blue' makes a striking focal point above a carpet of New Zealand burrs (*Acaena anserinifolia*), insignificant in flower but outstanding with their blue-grey foliage and pinkish-brown burrs.

▼ **Weeping cedar** The Atlas cedar (*Cedrus atlantica*) is a large, fast-growing conifer. However, its cultivar 'Glauca Pendula' is a superb small tree with pendulous branches thickly clothed with blue-green leaves. It forms a splendid background for a pool rimmed with blue and white irises.

CHOOSING TREES

The right choice of tree can enhance every garden, adding height, impact and perspective to even the smallest plot.

In order to achieve the distinctive appeal of maturity, a garden should contain at least one tree, and ideally two or three. A garden without trees is severely lacking in height and backbone. A tree becomes a focal point – its size, shape and colour dominating a garden, enhancing its good points and concealing inferior aspects.

You may decide not to plant any trees because you think they will take too long to grow. This is a mistake. By careful selection, a tree can be found for every garden, however small or awkward, and although some trees take time to reach their mature shape, there is immeasurable pleasure in watching a young tree develop. Decid-uous trees provide interesting colour and form throughout the year – from the moment the swelling buds are succeeded by leaves, flowers, fruit and autumn tints, through to the winter display of bare branches and attractive bark.

Evergreens – broad-leaved trees and conifers – come into their own in winter when they continue to add life and colour to the slumbering garden, and shelter for the native bird population.

Economically it's a good idea to avoid short-term effects. Young plants are much cheaper to buy than those grown on to larger size in a nursery. They also settle down much more quickly when planted.

▲ **Balm of Gilead poplar** An outstanding specimen tree, the variegated form (*Populus* × *candicans* 'Aurora') has creamy-white marbled foliage, tinged pink on young leaves.

▼ **Japanese angelica tree** This small ornamental tree (*Aralia elata* 'Variegata') bears arching foliage sprays edged with creamy-white.

In a small garden, some trees – even those that reach only 7.5m (25ft) in height – should be avoided as they cast too much shade or dominate the garden. Height and spread without excess weight are the most important considerations; some of the maples and crab apples with their rounded heads of lightweight foliage are ideal for the smaller garden, and rarely outgrow their allotted space.

Sometimes, too, the root systems of trees can create major problems. Willows, for instance, have long roots which, in their search for water and nutrients, can penetrate and extensively damage drains. The roots of large trees planted too close to buildings and walls can severely affect their foundations. On clay soils, particularly during prolonged drought, the amount of water taken up by trees can cause subsidence.

Feature trees
Specimen trees are those grown in isolation and positioned as focal points in lawns, as corner features in paved gardens or close to a vista. Therefore, the selection and placing of these trees is especially important. When planting, also

take into account the ultimate height and spread of specimen trees.

When choosing a tree the most important factors to consider are its size and shape, and the quality of its foliage. Trees bearing

▲ **Shade trees** Mature trees lightly shade an incomparable colour association of vivid blue and soft yellow. Tall *Meconopsis betonicifolia* tower impressively above eye-catching *Primula florindae* and blue-grey *Hosta sieboldiana*.

► **Weeping silver birch** Ideal for the small garden, *Betula pendula* 'Youngii' trails its slender branches and pale green foliage as a backdrop for spring daffodils and early tulips.

22

▲ **Golden rain** Laden with cascading sprays of golden-yellow pea-flowers, the golden rain tree (*Laburnum*) blooms in late spring and early summer. It is a popular choice for small gardens although parts of the tree, especially the seeds, are poisonous.

attractive flowers and fruit are a popular choice. Soil and position, exposure to wind and frost hardiness are also significant factors, especially when contemplating a specimen tree. Having made a selection, the next step is to give the tree the best possible conditions, so that it will thrive and flourish over the years.

Deciduous trees are best planted during the dormant season, although container-grown specimen trees can be planted at almost any time. All need good, fertile soil and plenty of water in the early years until a good root system has become established. All trees should be firmly staked and secured with proper tree ties.

Tree shapes
Trees come in many shapes and sizes so be sure to choose the right ones, especially when growing specimen trees in a garden where space is at a premium. Select slender upright species which add height without smothering other plants. For a more relaxing effect a tree of spreading habit may be preferable. Low branches impede access in a confined area and can be a nuisance when moving, but are ideal for providing shade — over woodland plants, for example. Since young trees rarely reflect their eventual mature shape, check their development with the nursery before buying.

Upright shapes The strong vertical accent of a tall, green column would be ideal for some gardens, but too formal for others. Upright forms of many popular trees are suitable for planting in a small garden – their tidy growth creates little shade and doesn't take up too much space. The upright forms of the Japanese cherry *Prunus* 'Amanogawa' or the crab apple *Malus tschonoskii* are good examples.

Weeping shapes Pendulous trees have become popular in small gardens where their controlled outlines are particularly effective. It's best to avoid the weeping willow (*Salix alba* 'Tristis') as it is so beautiful as a young tree it is easy to forget how thirsty its roots are and how much space it requires. The willow-leaved pear (*Pyrus salicifolia* 'Pendula'), a small weeping tree with creamy blossom and silvery foliage, is a much better choice.

The ornamental cherry *Prunus subhirtella* 'Pendula Rubra' is another good choice for the small garden. Its clusters of pink, spring flowers are followed by dense drooping foliage that turn brilliant colours in autumn.

The graceful growth habit of the silver birch (*Betula pendula*), with its light and airy foliage, is ideal for planting individually as a specimen or as part of a group. For the small garden, look for the form 'Youngii', which maintains a manageable height.

Round shapes If you only have room for one tree, you may prefer one with a simple round crown. One of the best small trees with a neat, rounded shape is the ornamental thorn (*Crataegus × prunifolia*). This handsome tree has attractive flowers which are followed in autumn by haws and colourful foliage, and will make a fine feature in a lawn.

The maple family includes many trees with pleasant, rounded shapes. One of the most striking is the sycamore (*Acer pseudoplatanus* 'Brilliantissimum'). Its curved outline is highlighted by the coral pink of its young foliage, which changes to pale green as it matures. The sweet gum (*Liquidambar styraciflua*) is often mistaken for a maple. Young trees have a conical shape, but mature trees develop domed crowns. It is especially lovely in autumn when it may be orange, red or purple. The stag's horn sumach (*Rhus typhina*) with its velvety bark and vibrant foliage is also attractive in autumn, but has a smaller, more pendulous shape.

Coloured foliage

Trees with strikingly coloured foliage are particularly suitable for specimen planting. Purple and golden members of the *Acer* family are invaluable. Other golden-leaved trees, such as the false acacia (*Robinia pseudoacacia* 'Frisia'), can add colour to the garden, as will the coppery, young leaves of the Indian bean tree (*Catalpa bignonioides* 'Aurea').

For variegated leaf colour choose the small Japanese angelica tree (*Aralia elata* 'Variegata') which is valued for its handsome, large pinnate leaves heavily margined with creamy-white.

For a really spectacular effect, try the copper beech (*Fagus sylvatica* 'Purpurea') – it bears leaves in a variety of shades of red, ranging from a light red to a magnificent deep, intense copper.

▲ **Sweet gum tree**
Outstanding for its blazing autumn colours, the sweet gum (*Liquidambar styraciflua*) grows like a slender, upright pyramid of glossy dark green, maple-like leaves.

◄ **Japanese maple** The slow-growing and spreading *Acer japonicum* 'Aureum' is splendid for small gardens. It does best in light shade where its golden-yellow foliage can't be harmed by sun scorch. The Japanese maple is tolerant of lime in the soil.

Flowering trees

There are many fine trees among the flowering almond and cherry (*Prunus*) group. The ornamental weeping cherry (*Prunus subhirtella*) is one of the best spring-flowering trees.

The widely planted laburnum or golden rain tree (*Laburnum × watereri* 'Vossii') is suitable for any medium-sized garden. Its drooping golden flowers form a wonderful display in late spring and early summer. However, as it is very poisonous – especially the seeds – avoid planting it in places where young children are likely to play.

▲ Deciduous azaleas Of almost tree-like proportions, deciduous azaleas flower in late spring and make admirable specimen plants for small gardens. They associate well with bluebells; in autumn their foliage develops red and golden tints which can be reflected in an underplanting of goblet-shaped colchicums.

◄ Winter cheer The ground beneath the bare branches of deciduous trees is ideal for small, late-winter and early-spring flowering bulbs. Winter aconites (*Eranthis hyemalis*) raise green-ruffed, golden flower globes while the lilac *Crocus tomasinianus* is one of the first crocuses to come into bloom. Dainty pink *Cyclamen coum* complete a display of pastel colours.

25

Of all the flowering trees few can rival the magnolias for majestic beauty. Some need plenty of room to show to advantage, but the small *Magnolia stellata* is easily fitted into most gardens.

Many fruiting plants give great value for money since their superb flowering display is followed by wonderful fruits in late summer or autumn. The crab apple *Malus* 'John Downie' is an exceptionally good example of a tree with pleasant blossom and orange/scarlet fruit.

The mountain ash group (*Sorbus* species and varieties) is an important genus of trees which have a long flowering season as well as an extended display of brilliantly coloured fruits. *Sorbus aucuparia* 'Beissneri' has, in addition, striking foliage colour in autumn.

Evergreen trees
For year-round foliage, choose from a large selection of evergreen trees. Holly (species and varieties of *Ilex*) has many variegated forms. Some are silver or golden, while a few are more symmetrically shaped than those found in the wild. Holly is very slow-growing so, even when it is mature, it remains a manageable height and is easily trimmed to the right size and shape.

The Australian eucalypts (*Eucalyptus*), better known as gum trees, are very popular. The great advantage of these trees is that their foliage is fairly sparse, so they don't cast dense shade. Some are not fully hardy – the alpine snow gum (*Eucalyptus niphophila*), a slow-growing species with beautiful mottled bark and large, leathery grey-green leaves, is the hardiest variety. The popular cider gum tree (*Eucalyptus gunnii*) is also hardy and is often cut back each year to the size of a shrub. Its attractive, blue-green or silvery-white foliage is much prized by flower arrangers. Left unpruned, it grows very quickly into a spear-shaped tree, increasing in size by 90-180cm (3-6ft) a year.

The strawberry tree (*Arbutus unedo*) is another attractive evergreen with white or pink autumn flowers. It is so slow-growing that it is suitable for small gardens.

Conifers
Many conifers grow to the size of forest trees and are therefore unsuitable for small gardens. Some columnar shapes, however, such as *Chamaecyparis lawsoniana* 'Columnaris', the slender *Juniperus communis* 'Hibernica', or the golden Irish yew (*Taxus baccata* 'Fastigiata Aureomarginata') make admirable specimen trees.

Dwarf conifers are the mainstay of many small gardens. They come in a wide range of shapes and colours, and are ideal for planting among heathers in the rock garden or individually, as part of a lawn group.

▼ **Fruit trees** Shade-loving plants, such as blue and white bell flowers (*Campanula persicifolia*) and red and purple foxgloves, turn a mature apple tree into a stunning focal point.

◄ **Snow gum tree** Most evergreens cast dense permanent shade which makes it impossible for anything to grow beneath them. The eucalypts or gum trees, however, are generally well-branched with long and narrow leaves that allow light to filter through. The fast-growing snowgum (*Eucalyptus niphophila*) is one of the hardiest species, weathering hard frosts better than it does strong winds.

Cool colours complement its near-white trunk, and suitable companions include ground-covering dead nettle (*Lamium maculatum* 'Beacon Silver') with its neat, silvery, evergreen leaves, and the grey-green dense foliage of the shrubby *Euphorbia characias*. In early spring, its pale yellow flower bracts add a splash of colour to the scene.

► **Laburnum tunnel** Many stately gardens make a feature of laburnum walks where the trees are plaited and trained to form a tunnel of cascading golden-yellow blooms in late spring and early summer.

The effect is spectacular, especially in association with an underplanting of rose-purple ornamental onions (*Allium rosenbachianum*) which flower at the same time. Such pleasing partnerships, on a smaller scale, can easily be achieved in more modest gardens.

▶ **Star magnolia** The slow-growing *Magnolia stellata* begins to flower while still quite young, opening its fragrant white flowers to form wide stars in mid spring. The many-petalled blooms have faint traces of purple at the base of the petals — a colour theme picked up in an underplanting of bergenias. Their glossy green foliage thrives quite happily in the shade cast by the magnolia's summer canopy.

▼ **Floral carpet** In spite of its Mediterranean origin, the hardy little *Cyclamen hederifolium* thrives and colonizes in the rich soil and moist shade found beneath deciduous trees and shrubs. The mauve, pink and white flowers appear from late summer through to early winter and are handsomely offset by dark green, silver marbled leaves.

AUTUMN COLOURS

**With careful planning and planting,
a glorious autumn show of leaves and berries
can follow on from summer.**

Autumn is one of the most beautiful times of the year. The dying leaves of deciduous trees and shrubs blaze with colour, and fruits and berries add brilliant hues of red, yellow, orange, white and purple to the scene. With a wide range of cultivated plants to choose from, it is easy to plan your garden so that summer's vivid flowers are followed by a brilliant autumn display.

Only in the largest gardens can a whole area be devoted solely to an autumn show. For average and small gardens, choose compact plants that are attractive for weeks or even months, rather than brief spells. Aim to blend those that look spectacular in autumn with plants that are outstanding in flower or foliage at other times of the year.

When choosing a plant, weigh its autumn appearance against the way it looks during the rest of the year. Some, such as snowy mespilus (*Amelanchier canadensis*), deciduous azaleas (*Rhododendron*), ornamental cherries (*Prunus*) and crab apples (*Malus*) have attractive spring flowers as well as striking autumn foliage or berries (or both). Others, such as *Parrotia persica*, are relatively dull except for their extremely brief autumn show. And some, such as *Liquidambar, Ginkgo* and tulip tree (*Liriodendron*), are beautiful but much too large for the average garden.

Every category of plant, from trees, shrubs and climbers to perennials, biennials (such as autumn and winter flowering pansies), annuals and bulbs, can be represented in the autumn garden. Most people carefully organize their autumn garden in order to obtain a good balance of colourful flowers, foliage and fruit or berries.

Leaves

You only have to cast your eye across a hillside covered with birch, beech or maple to know that autumn leaf colour is the most dramatic visual aspect of the season. Equally beautiful autumn foliage 'vignettes' can be created in the garden. The 'Heptalobum' group of Japanese maples, many deciduous berberis, viburnums and cotoneasters, hardy plumbago, smoke bush (*Cotinus*), dogwoods (*Cornus*) and ornamental blueberries (*Vaccinium*), vines and currants are all recommended. If space permits, include plants that will give a range of colours. For yellow, there's birch or beech, for vivid reds *Euonymus alatus* 'Compactus', *Berberis thunbergii* or *Acer palmatum*, and for orange the brilliantly coloured sumach (*Rhus typhina*) or *Fothergilla monticola*.

As leaf fall is inevitably followed by bare branches, consider the shape and bark colour of a deciduous tree or shrub. Those with an attractive winter pre-

▲ **Autumn cones** Although cones are not as striking as fruits and foliage, they are a valuable feature of the autumn scene. Cones vary in shape, size and texture and their subtle colours are welcome in any display.

▼ **Foliage colours** Red, orange, gold, russet and yellow are all present in this dramatic autumn display. Colour is affected by climatic variations, a warm and cloudy autumn often resulting in dull leaf colours.

sence, such as birches, acers, *Rhus*, willows and some of the dogwoods, are well worth including.

Berries, fruit and seed pods
The other major source of autumn colour apart from foliage is fruit – a vast colour range is available, and some plants produce massive clusters of berries which completely obliterate the leaves and stems. Cotoneasters and pyracanthas – red, orange and yellow-berried forms – are extremely popular. Other options include the translucent red berries of the guelder rose (*Viburnum opulus*), set off to perfection by bright yellow autumn leaves, or the red, orange, white or pink berry clusters of the various kinds of mountain ash (*Sorbus*).

Most crab apples and flowering quinces have an attractive shape as well as interesting foliage, flowers and fruit. Chinese lanterns, however, although fascinating to look at in late summer, have insignificant flowers, dull foliage, and a sprawling, invasive growth habit.

Specialist rose nurseries stock a diverse range of old-fashioned shrub roses with many different shapes and colours of hips. There are roses with huge round hips, flask-shaped hips, hips carried in sprays or clusters, and hips ranging in colour from clear orange to deepest crimson and even black.

Conifer cones – usually more subtly coloured than flowers, fruit and foliage – also add interest. Sizes vary from the huge cones of

the European silver fir, standing like candles along the branches, to the delicate, flower-like cones of larch; colours vary from the pinkish red of *Picea likiangensis* to the blue black of *Abies forrestii*.

The seed heads of silky yellow-flowered *Clematis tangutica* and *C. orientalis*, and the old-fashioned silver circles of honesty, offer subtle autumn tones. And a large clump of pampas grass will make an effective autumnal focal point on a lawn.

Consider how long a plant will put on a good autumn show. Delicate seed pods are vulnerable to storms, and brilliantly coloured autumn leaves, such as those of spindle, may only last a few days as a backdrop for the fruits. Generally, persistent fruits are

▲ **Pool reflections** Richly coloured autumn foliage is mirrored dramatically in the still waters of a pool. In the garden, trees and shrubs should be sited well away from pools otherwise the leaves will foul the water and clog up pumps.

▲ ▶ **Seed pods** The native spindle tree (*Euonymus europaeus*) is weighed down in autumn with clusters of seed pods — the variety 'Red Cascade' are rosy-red.

▶ **Ornamental vine** The attractive foliage of the fruiting *Vitis* 'Brant' changes colour spectacularly from the rich green of summer to shades of golden-yellow, dark red and purple in autumn.

▲ **Japanese maples** The rounded form and divided leaves of Japanese maple *Acer palmatum* 'Dissectum' are more distinctive in autumn when clothed in hues of yellow, orange and red.

better value in the garden than those which quickly disappear. Many hawthorns, for example, hold their fruits well into winter.

Ornamental fruit colour
Most ornamental fruits and berries are in the orange-red range. The colours vary in intensity, from bright and luminous, to deeper and less eye-catching shades. Generally, a background of paler or darker foliage helps them to stand out more than a green of the same degree of intensity.

Dark blue, dark purple or black ornamental fruits can be beautiful when viewed at proximity, and are excellent for flower arranging.

Generally, however, dark fruits make little impact when seen from a distance. Dark fruits with a pale, waxy bloom, such as mahonia and some berberis, appear more prominent when they are seen against deep green foliage.

White or light-coloured berries can be eye-catching, especially when they are set against a con-

trasting backdrop. For example, the pale fruit produced by snowberries or yellow *Cotoneaster* 'Rothschildianus' is particularly striking when seen against a sombre yew hedge.

Unripe green berries tend to blend with the surrounding greenery. They make much more impact when they are set against red, purple or yellow foliage.

Fruiting partners
The autumn foliage of some plants creates a perfect setting for their own fruits or pods – for example, fishbone cotoneaster (*Cotoneaster horizontalis*) has crimson autumn foliage and scarlet berries.

Evergreen and semi-evergreen plants provide their own foliage backdrop. However, deciduous

▼ **Rose hips** The arching branches of *Rosa moyesii* 'Geranium' are attractively adorned with bright red flowers in high summer. The autumn display of drooping, crimson, flask-shaped hips is equally spectacular.

fruiting plants which retain their fruits after they have lost their leaves need carefully chosen partners. For example, the bright red berry spikes of lords-and-ladies (*Arum italicum*) look more effective rising out of a ground-cover of ivy or vinca than emerging from dead leaves or bare earth.

Try to avoid potential clashes when an ornamental fruiting plant is wall-trained, or displayed against a wall. Orange and red berries can clash with red brick-work, especially if it is new, but they will often look attractive set against mellow or pale brickwork, rendering, or natural stone. They also look good against dark or light wooden fences.

Yellow and white berries are best set against dark brickwork, stone or wood; they tend to blend in with pale backgrounds and so disappear from view.

Site plants with ornamental fruits where they can be seen from house windows. Plants can be trained to overhang certain windows, so their fruit-laden branches frame the view outwards.

Fruiting plants are also effective when planted near paths and patios, and can be used to make a pretty framework for the entrance to a garden, porch or front door.

Some low-growing evergreen fruiting plants, such as gaultheria and bearberry, make excellent ground-cover. Try pernettyas and butcher's broom in a mixed border or wild garden.

▲ **Pure honesty** The oval seed pods of honesty (*Lunaria annua*) are so transparent that the seeds show through them. For dried flower arrangements, peel off the outer covering and remove the black seeds.

► **Crab apples** Resplendent in late spring, crab apples (*Malus* sp.) bear massed clusters of single or double, white, pink or red flowers. They reach a second high point in autumn when their branches are laden with fruit. The white-flowered 'John Downie' is one of the finest fruiting cultivars, bearing large conical apples which ripen through yellow and pink to bright orange and crimson.

◄ **Chinese lanterns** The bright orange seed pods of *Physalis alkekengi* are wonderfully long-lasting in dried flower arrangements. However, in leaf and flower, these hardy perennials have little ornamental value, and they are extremely invasive and self-seeding.

▲ **Guelder rose** The maple-like Guelder rose (*Viburnum opulus* 'Compactum') is a wide-spreading deciduous shrub with white flower heads in summer. In autumn, it bears long-lasting, bright red berries.

▼ **Blue barberry** The evergreen *Berberis darwinii* with its glossy, holly-like foliage is outstanding throughout the year. In late spring it bears clusters of rich yellow flowers, followed in autumn by waxy blue berries.

▼ **Mountain ash** Related to our native species, *Sorbus hupehensis* is an elegant, small tree with blue-green leaves that turn brilliant orange in autumn. Drooping clusters of white berries develop in late summer.

Plants with pendent ornamental fruit, such as *Leycesteria formosa* and ornamental vines, are ideally sited where they can be viewed from below. Ornamental vines could be trained to cover a pergola situated over a patio or path, and *Leycesteria formosa* would look effective grown in a raised bed.

Pollinating partners

The primary function of berry colour is to attract birds, which then eat the berries and distribute the seed, thus increasing the species' chance of survival. Birds' tastes vary, and locality, availability of other nearby food and weather conditions also affect which berries are likely to get eaten. Berries of certain plants, such as skimmia and ivy, are often left alone. Others, such as rowan, tend to disappear immediately.

Some plants, such as sea buckthorn, skimmia, butcher's broom, aucuba and many hollies, are either male or female. Approximately one male plant is needed to pollinate three females and thereby ensure crops of berries. Garden centres should specify the sex of plants where relevant, so check labels carefully.

Some plants such as laurustinus and arbutus for example, only

▲ **Red-barked dogwood** The easily grown *Cornus alba* 'Sibirica' with its bright red stems, looks striking in the company of *Euonymus fortunei* 'Emerald 'n' Gold' tinged with pink as winter approaches.

▼ **Firethorn** The evergreen *Pyracantha* grows well in any soil and site. Its creamy flowers in early summer are followed by clusters of berries; yellow-berried forms retain their fruits better than red-berried types.

◄ **Shades of red** The spindle tree, *Euonymus europaeus* 'Red Cascade', provides a range of red hues in autumn. As the green foliage turns purplish red, the crimson seed pods split open to reveal glossy orange fruits.

▼ **Stinking iris** Its pale purple summer flowers are insignificant and marred by a rank smell emitted from its evergreen leaves, but *Iris foetidissima* redeems itself in autumn when the large green pods peel back to display rows of orange-scarlet seeds. The fruiting stems are excellent for dried flower arrangements.

fruit in extremely favourable conditions. Many conifers and some broad-leaved trees such as magnolias produce cones and fruits only when they are mature. Dwarf conifers rarely bear cones.

Many plants fruit on young wood, and regular pruning is liable to remove the following year's display. This often happens with mature, wall-trained pyracantha, but a poor display one year is often compensated for by excellent shows in subsequent years.

Evergreen standbys

Evergreens, whether broad-leaved like elaeagnus, or coniferous like yews and junipers, are as important in autumn as they are in winter. Some of the smaller conifers – for example *Juniperus horizontalis* – take on bronze, purplish or red colouring in colder weather, thus adding valuable autumn and winter interest.

There are also conifer cones which add subtle interest to the garden in winter. They range from the huge, upright cones of the noble fir to the delicate cones of larch and cryptomeria. Most cones develop from green to brown or silvery grey, but there are white, orange, blue, violet and nearly black varieties. Some will remain on the tree for at least a year or more before falling.

Don't forget evergreen perennials, such as Christmas rose (*Helleborus niger*) and *Euphorbia robbiae*; and trailers such as *Euonymus fortunei* 'Coloratus', whose dark green leaves take on

rich, red tones in autumn. Even the common ivy can take on red tones in cold weather.

Using autumn colour

Brilliant autumn colours contrast well against light or dark backgrounds, such as a whitewashed wall or a yew hedge. Choose background settings carefully: a crimson Japanese maple seen against red brickwork, or a yellow field maple set agaisnt ochre-yellow bricks looks extremely garish.

However, one of the joys of

autumn planting is that there is scope to experiment. Try grouping eye-catching colours roughly equal in size and regularly spaced apart to form a focal point; or break up autumn colour into paint-like dabs – the tiny ivy-leaved cyclamen set in pink drifts under a tree; or use colour as exclamation points – a magnificent specimen tulip tree, or clump of maples on a lawn. Virginia creeper (*Parthenocissus*) can be trained to cover a house – the effect is truly breathtaking.

Shrub partners

Shrubs form the essence of every garden, creating a permanent backdrop for ever-changing groups of bulbs, herbaceous perennials and annuals. Their floral displays, autumn tints and berry colours alter through the year with the seasons.

Many shrubs are chosen for their flowering qualities, but it can be a mistake to judge a shrub solely on the short time it is in bloom. Foliage can be of greater importance as it is present for many months. Leaves come in a variety of shades, not only green, but also silver, grey, gold and purple. Leaf shape and texture range from the miniscule foliage of brooms to the huge leaves of fatsia, and from the leathery rhododendron to the ferny leaves of bladder senna.

Some shrubs are best seen in isolation, while others are best integrated in mixed borders with other shrubs or perennials. This creates opportunities for establishing associations that harmonize in colour and contrast pleasingly in form. With careful selection, a group of plants can maintain interest for months if their flowering displays overlap. The autumn season offers fresh delights with seasonal colours and fruit.

Climbing shrubs are invaluable for clothing walls and fences with greenery and flowers and for extending the garden from the horizontal plane to the vertical. Clematis and roses make charming companions and ivy is a particularly useful partner for more flamboyant if temporary climbers.

Roses, with their rich colours and diversity of form, are particular garden favourites. They are sometimes grown in beds of their own, but are most outstanding in mixed borders or as specimen shrubs. They thrive in the company of delphiniums and lilies, lavender and irises and they flower unceasingly in pots and patio beds and clamber up walls and pillars.

Shrub companions *Lavatera olbia* and purple *Buddleia davidii* create a spectacular long-flowering association.

SHRUB HARMONY

Shrubs play an important role in the garden, strongly supported by other varieties and species of plants.

Today's gardens are usually too small for an old-fashioned shrubbery, but shrubs are still essential for a garden's structure. They give height, weight and substance to other plantings and provide interest throughout the year. Whether used as specimens, as background or as focal points in mixed borders, shrubs should be grouped to bring out the best from their varying colours and forms.

Although shrubs are usually chosen for their floral displays, these often last for only a relatively short period. The show of foliage is of much longer duration – in some deciduous shrubs, the

unfolding of their leaves in spring and their rich colouring in autumn paint pictures of particular beauty. In addition to the seasonal aspect, leaves in every conceivable shade of green are in evidence all year round.

Even more arresting are those shrubs with variegated leaves in shades of pink, grey, silver and yellow, as well as those with coloured foliage, from the purple smoke trees to the gold of *Lonicera nitida* 'Baggesen's Gold', the grey-leaved hebes and the silvery senecios.

Evergreens do not go through seasonal colour changes, but they

▲ **Cool colours** Pure white, orange-scented flowers of *Philadelphus* 'Beauclerk' and yellow lupin-like spires of *Thermopsis montana* rise from a sea of ice-blue *Veronica teucrium*.

▼ **Shades of pink** The purple-leaved smoke tree (*Cotinus coggygria* 'Purpureus') makes a dramatic background for purple-pink *Rodgersia pinnata* and pink *Astrantia maxima*.

◄ **Woodland associates** In cool, moist soil and dappled shade, woodland shrubs such as rhododendrons and azaleas burst into riotous colour during late spring and early summer. Here, the fiery, orange-red trumpets of an azalea are tempered by the cool, yellow globes of *Trollius × hybridus.*

▼ **Evergreen gold** The ulta-hardy spindle tree (*Euonymus fortunei* 'Emerald 'n' Gold') shines like a beacon on the dullest day. It forms a dense dwarf shrub which glows next to the sombre colour of a false cypress, more so in winter when the gold and cream foliage takes on pinkish tones. In high summer, blue and white *Viola cornuta*, fringed pinks and white-flowered *Geranium pratense* 'Kashmir White' add their cottage garden charm.

◄ **Beauty bush** Aptly named, the deciduous *Kolkwitzia amabilis* appears like a rippling fountain in early summer when a profusion of porcelain-pink flowers decorates its arching branches. Such beauty needs little embellishment, but a foreground of upright foxgloves (*Digitalis purpurea*) is a perfect complement in colour and shape. In autumn, the shrub's purple and brown leaves could be teamed with autumn crocus (*Colchicum speciosum*).

display rich diversity in leaf form, ranging from the huge fan-like leaves of fatsias to the needle-like sprays of heathers and the miniscule leaves of various cotoneasters and berberis. They add both life and colour to the winter garden, and several varieties give delight with their colourful clusters of berries and fruit.

Choosing shrubs

In the final selection, flower colour is likely to be one of the main reasons for choosing one particular shrub rather than another. Luckily, the range of shrubs is so great that it is possible to find a flowering variety for every month of the year, from the winter-flowering witch hazels (*Hamamelis* sp.) through a vast choice of spring, summer and autumn-flowering types to Christmas-blooming camellias and ericas whose bright colours last for several months from late autumn into the early spring.

However, even when flower colour is the primary consideration, some thought should be given to a shrub's overall appearance and performance. Forsythia, for example, is one of our brightest and best loved spring shrubs, but once its golden flowers have finished, it holds little attraction, with nondescript leaves and a tendency to grow leggy and gaunt unless pruned hard back every year.

Such shrubs should be sited in a position where their blossom can be enjoyed in full while their form is hidden by other, more interesting companions during the rest of the year.

In general, garden shrubs should be an equal mixture of deciduous types and evergreen varieties, with a proportion of conifers and shrubs with coloured foliage for contrast.

Grouping shrubs

Some shrubs are so outstanding in flower, leaf and form that they deserve a prominent position where they can be enjoyed all year round. Typical examples are the shrubby acers, especially the Japanese types like *Acer japonicum* 'Aureum' with its deeply lobed and broad, yellow leaves that turn brilliant red and orange in autumn, and the weeping butterfly bush (*Buddleia alternifolia*) whose slender branches arch gracefully to form a rippling,

sweet-scented flower fountain in early summer.

Other shrubs make a much greater impact when planted in groups of three – the variegated elaeagnus, for example, with their gold-splashed evergreen leaves, are visually more impressive as a

▼ **The lime-haters** Given acid soil, light shade and protection from strong winds, a shrubbery of mixed rhododendrons and azaleas is a stunning sight in late spring. Although available in a wide range of colours, these shrubs look most spectacular when colours and shapes are chosen with restraint.

▲ **Signs of spring** The ubiquitous but indispensable forsythia is the earliest of the spring-flowering shrubs, bursting into a mass of golden-yellow blooms before the first leaf has unfolded. It is accompanied here by the dainty, clear pink blossom of flowering cherry (*Prunus sargentii*). At ground level a sprawling Japanese quince (*Chaenomeles* × *superba* 'Crimson and Gold') adds colour to the spring scene.

◄ **Pink on pink** The climbing *Actinidia kolomikta* bears white, lightly scented flowers in early summer. The shrub, however, is more remarkable for the tri-coloured leaf variegations found on mature plants, where the top half of each leaf is creamy-white flushed with pink. It forms a spectacular backcloth for the rich pink, semi-double flowers of the Rugosa rose 'Roseraie de l'Hay'.

► **Mop-head hortensias** Varieties of mop-headed hydrangeas (*Hydrangea macrophylla*) turn out pink or red on alkaline soils, unless heavily dosed with bluing powders. The splendid 'Générale Vicomtesse de Vibraye' is a naturally vivid rose colour, which deepens as the flower heads mature. The colour change looks magnificent in high summer, seen here against a background of the rambler rose 'Dorothy Perkins', whose tall stems are weighed down with festoons of double, blush-pink blooms.

▼ **Wall protection** The common myrtle (*Myrtus communis*), so prolific in Mediterranean regions, is not reliably hardy in Britain, although it will generally succeed when given the protection of a warm, sunny wall. Here, the evergreen shrub will form a mound of dark green, glossy and aromatic leaves, decorated in summer with fragrant white flowers with golden, star-like stamens.

   Myrtle looks best when partnered with other evergreen shrubs that thrive in the same sheltered conditions. In front is a dark green, leathery-leaved *Pittosporum tobira*, whose fragrant white flowers mature through cream to butter-yellow. Sprawling in the foreground, clumps of the silver-leaved *Senecio* 'Sunshine' add their bright yellow daisy flowers.

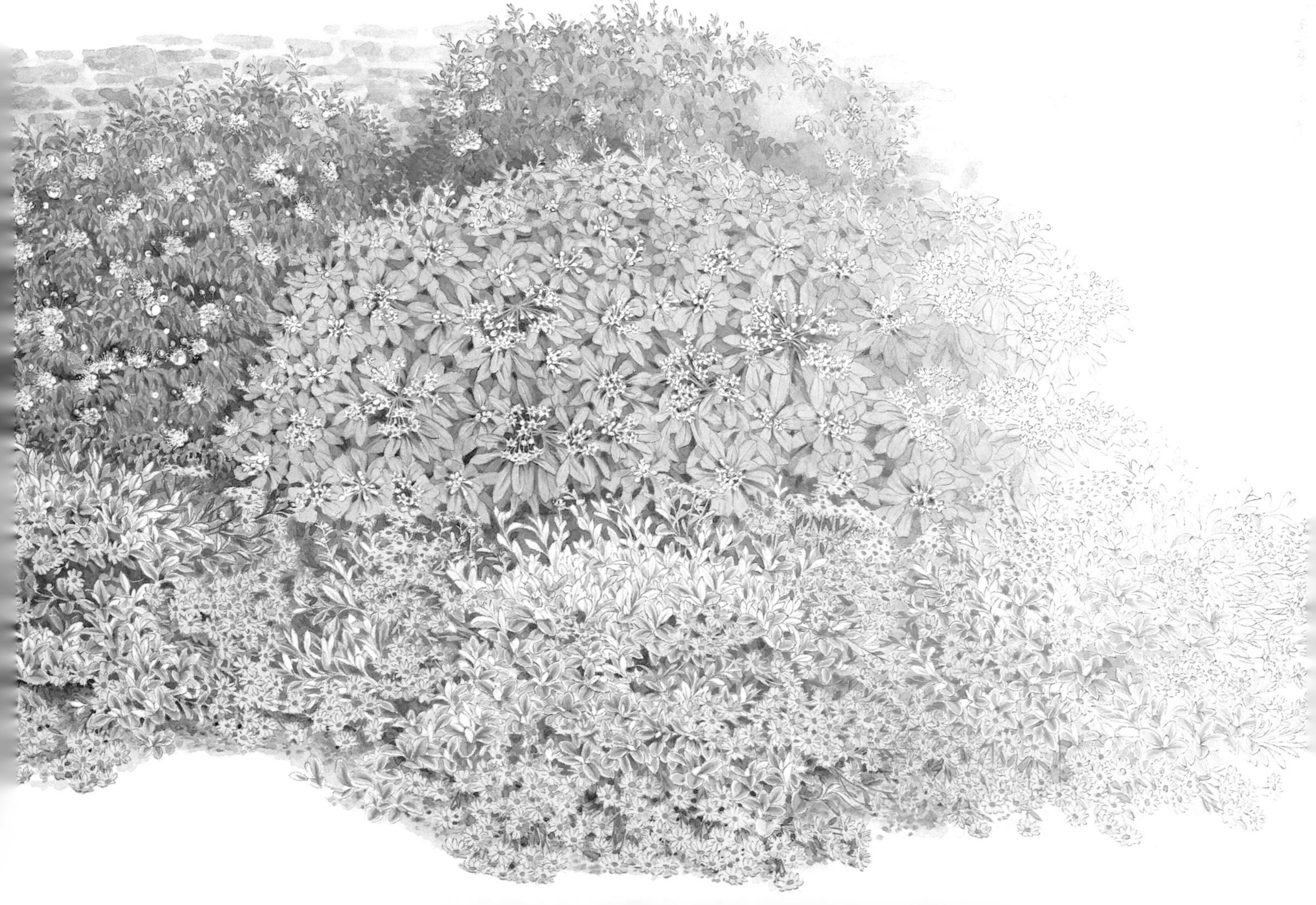

▲ **Snow in summer** The popular snowball bush (*Viburnum opulus* 'Sterile', also listed as 'Roseum') is adorned in late spring and early summer with 'snowballs' of creamy-white, which appear striking among the dark green, maple-like leaves that colour richly in autumn.
  Such solidity is lightened by the airy gracefulness of pink-flowered tamarisk (*Tamarix parviflora*), whose branches are clothed with fluffy plumes of deep pink flowers.

◄ **Grey and silver** Foliage shrubs are invaluable as foils for strong flower colours. Here, grey-leaved lavender (*Lavandula angustifolia* 'Hidcote') and silvery *Artemisia absinthium* 'Lambrook Silver' flank an old-fashioned Gallica rose, 'Rosa Mundi', magnificent with its crimson and white striped blooms. Clumps of silvery-grey white-flowered *Dianthus* 'Mrs Sinkins' create the perfect balance.

group in a mixed border than if they are dotted about singly. Shrubs with strongly coloured foliage, such as the purple smoke tree, can be overwhelming on their own, but when partnered by low-growing grey- or silver-leaved foliage plants, the effect is subdued and a picture of deliberate harmony is achieved.

In the same way, you can partner shrubs of contrasting outline or leaf form so that one highlights the other. Narrowly upright shrubs, such as the deciduous *Stranvaesia davidiana*, could be fronted by a hummock of evergreen *Viburnum davidii*, arching tamarisk by neat hebes and shrubby conifers with a carpet of heathers.

Shrub companions

Teaming shrubs with perennials, early or late-flowering bulbs, ground-covers and summer annuals adds to the elegance of the shrubs in flower and prolongs the season of interest.

Choose companion plants whose colours harmonize or contrast with those of the shrubs. Alternatively, select plants whose handsome, long-lasting foliage will draw attention away from the

nondescript leaves of some shrubs, and will also effectively hide any bareness around their feet.

Create spring scenes by planting clumps of naturalized narcissi underneath snowy mespilus (*Amelanchier lamarckii*) where the dainty white flowers will shimmer above the golden trumpets; or match them with the drooping catkins of the corkscrew hazel, with its curiously twisted twigs and foliage. You could also plant golden crocus or miniature blue irises at its feet.

Spring bulbs, too, are ideal for planting beneath deciduous shrubs grown for their vividly coloured bare winter stems – for example, plant white- or blue-striped crocuses, snowdrops or golden winter aconites beneath red-stemmed dogwood (*Cornus alba* 'Sibirica') or black-stemmed willow (*Salix gracilistyla* 'Melanostachys').

Stunning partnerships can be created where the flowering seasons of two shrubs overlap. Such associations work best when the flowers are within the same colour range. You could establish a long-lasting golden group by planting a creamy-yellow Warminster broom (*Cytisus* × *praecox*) next to a

▲ **Silver foil** The tender shrub *Pyrethrum ptarmaciflorum* is usually grown as a half-hardy annual. Its finely fretted, silvery leaves make a beautiful foil for the scarlet and purple bells of *Fuchsia* 'Mrs Popple'.

▼ **Fuchsia theme** The graceful variegated *Fuchsia magellanica* 'Versicolor' is in strong contrast to the bold foliage and stiff flower spikes of *Eucomis bicolor*.

white-flowered currant (*Ribes sanguineum* 'Album'). The broom comes into flower as the currant begins to fade, thus extending the floral display to a couple of months. Alternatively, partner the butter-yellow Jew's mallow (*Kerria japonica*), a graceful 1.5m (5ft) tall shrub, with the bridal wreath (*Spiraea × arguta*) with its dainty white flowers.

The magnificent rhododendrons are mainly regarded as specimen shrubs and woodland plants, but the smaller hybrid azaleas can be successfully integrated in mixed borders. The Kurume group is particularly suitable, being dwarf evergreens that are smothered in late spring with a profusion of bright or pastel flowers. A single plant, such as the crimson 'Beni Girl', the pink 'Hinomayo' or the white 'Kure no Yuki' ('Snowflake'), would make a spectacular focal point in a foliage grouping of ground-hugging cotoneasters and low *Euonymus fortunei* 'Silver Queen', with hostas and *Ajuga reptans* for ground-cover.

▲ **White and gold** The variegated evergreen shrub, *Euonymus fortunei* var. *radicans*, creates pools of light. Its companion is the American trout lily (*Erythronium revolutum* 'White Beauty') with its large mottled leaves and white, yellow-centred flowers.

▼ **White and red** North-facing sites can be problematic, but the climbing *Hydrangea petiolaris* thrives in such settings, bearing large clusters of greenish-white flowers in summer. The scarlet-flowered perennial *Tropaeolum speciosum* needs similar conditions.

◄ **Shrubby cinquefoils** The dainty *Potentilla fruticosa* is in flower for most of the summer. Here, it fronts a white and blue composition that includes tall, creamy-white *Aruncus dioicus* and steel-blue *Eryngium alpinum*. A flat-topped spiraea adds a touch of vibrant russet-red.

▲ **Height of summer** Yellow potentilla glows against *Lonicera nitida* 'Baggesen's Gold' and lavender-blue *Iris pallida*.

▼ **Depths of winter** *Fagus sylvatica* 'Purpurea Pendula', a golden juniper and *Hebe* 'Red Edge' stand silvered by frost.

▲ **Hanging basket** The frost-tender *Fuchsia* 'Marinka' with its deep red flowers is ideal for trailing over baskets in the company of blue lobelias.

◄ **Hardy fuchsias** The 30cm (12in) tall, red and mauve 'Tom Thumb' features in a daring combination with orange-red nasturtiums. Silver-grey *Santolina chamaecyparissus* has a calming effect.

▼ **Summer blues** The old fuchsia cultivar 'Mrs Popple' has retained its popularity and dominates this late-summer group with its blend of red, blue and purple colours. At the back are the arching branches of variegated *Fuchsia magellanica* 'Versicolor' and tall spikes of blue-flowered *Salvia farinacea*. An edging of prostrate *Campanula portenschlagiana* accentuates the blue in 'Mrs Popple'.

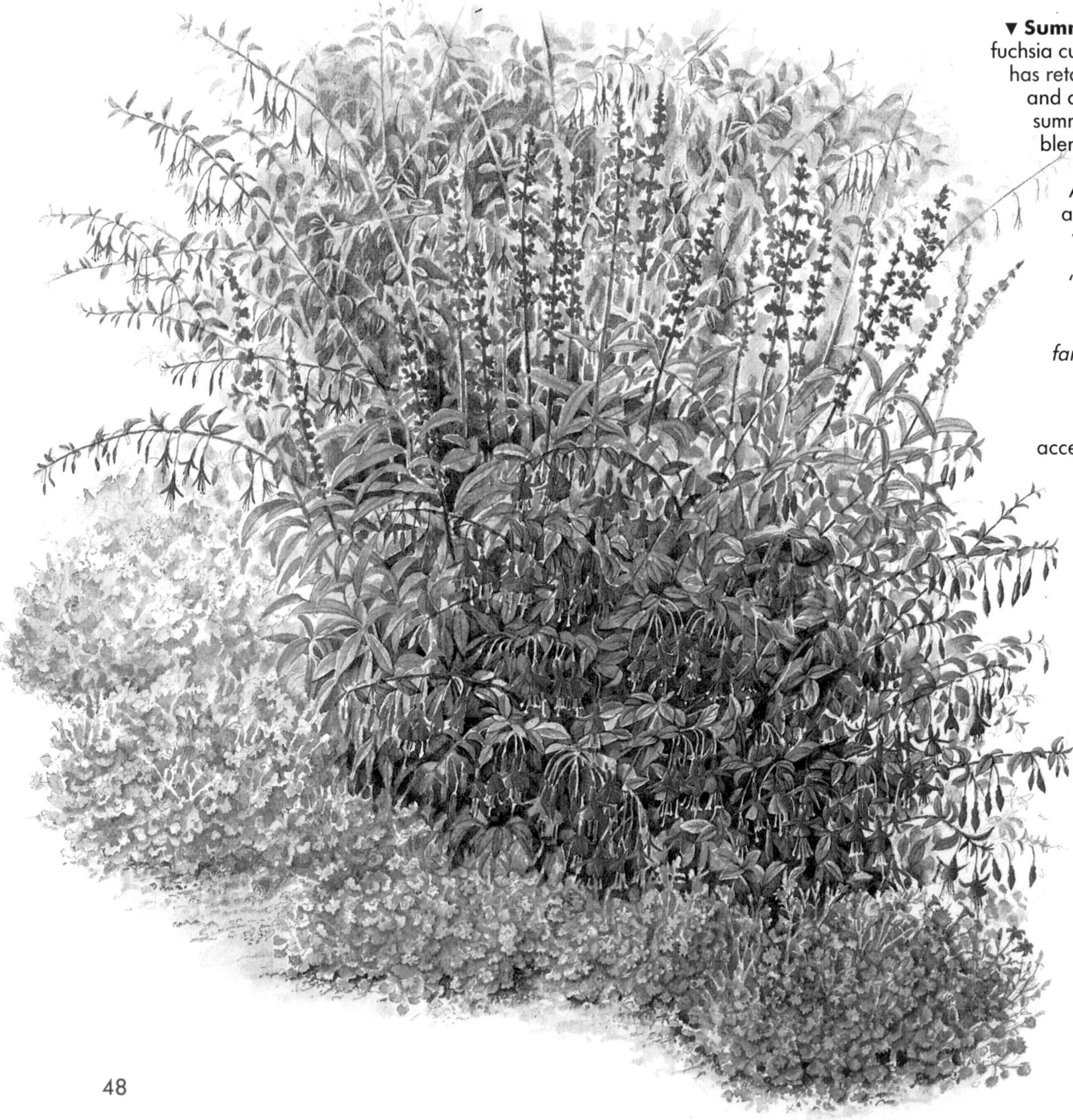

SMALL SHRUBS

Shrubs are the key to a garden that looks good all year round, and even the smallest area welcomes a selection of these hard-working plants.

Although brightly flowered perennials and annuals are important for colour and interest in the growing season – from late spring until the first autumn frosts – shrubs, whether evergreen or deciduous, are on show twelve months a year. Being permanent, they are particularly valuable from mid-autumn to mid-spring when they are the principal source of colour and texture. But whatever the season, shrubs give added depth and shape to the garden.

By choosing carefully, you can make the most of the year-round presence of shrubs. The majority are grown for their floral display and you can have shrubs in flower every month of the year. However, shrubs have much more to offer: brightly coloured berries or bark; unusual spring or autumn leaf colouring; fragrant flowers or aromatic leaves; evergreen foliage or, if deciduous, a winter framework of branches which often forms a lace-like tracery.

▲ **Rock roses** The low-growing *Cistus × lusitanicus* 'Decumbens' bears a succession of satiny, crimson-blotched flowers throughout high summer.

▼ **Summer shrubs** *Weigela florida* 'Foliis Purpureus' with its deep pink flowers and purple-flushed leaves, dominates a grouping of potentilla, golden spiraea and lavender.

▲ **Cinquefoil** Indispensable in the garden, the shrubby cinquefoils (*Potentilla fruticosa*) are ultra-hardy, neat of habit and tolerant of all types of soil. The dwarf cultivar 'Red Ace' grows best in light shade. It bears bright orange-red flowers from late spring into autumn.

▼ **Californian lilac** The evergreen *Ceanothus impressus*, although one of the hardiest of the ceanothus species, does best when situated against a sunny wall. The deep blue flowers of 'Puget Blue' glow above a footing of silver foliage.

▲ **Winter colours**
Dogwoods are most dramatic in winter when their bare, coloured branches bring life to a garden. Red-barked *Cornus alba* 'Sibirica' and yellow-stemmed *C. stolonifera* 'Flaviramea' must be pruned hard in spring to encourage new winter stems. Both have insignificant white flowers and dark green leaves (*below*).

Shrubs for small gardens

Where space is at a premium, it is best to choose shrubs which have several interesting features. The bright yellow winter flowers of *Mahonia aquifolium*, for example, are followed by blue-black berries in summer. These, combined with its glossy, evergreen leaves and architectural shape, make the shrub a focal point in the garden all year round.

Height and growth rate

The smaller the garden, the more important the choice of shrubs becomes. Always find out the potential height of a shrub *before* buying it. Some shrubs, such as holly and Portugal laurel (*Prunus lusitanica*), eventually become large trees if left to their own devices. However, with regular pruning they can remain shrubby for a number of years.

How quickly a shrub grows is as important as its ultimate height, so consider both factors together. Forsythias and camellias, for example, have much the same potential height (2.4m/8ft), but the former may take four or five years to reach it, the latter fifteen or twenty years. Eventually, many shrubs will lose their appeal with old age and are therefore best discarded.

Very often – particularly if the garden is relatively new – choosing shrubs becomes a balancing act: quick growth gives an established look to an otherwise bare plot of earth, but a shrub that outgrows its fair share of space within four or five years is a bad long-term choice.

Growing conditions – the amount of nutrients and moisture in the soil, sunlight, wind exposure and surrounding space available – affect both the height and growth rate of a shrub. The most extreme example is the art of bonsai, in which potentially huge trees are miniaturized by container growing, rigorous pruning and strict feeding regimes.

While it is impossible to attempt control on such a scale with garden shrubs, however small a garden, it is generally true that a shrub whose roots are confined grows more slowly than one with room to spread its roots. The same is true of shrubs growing in soil lacking in nutrients, but starving a shrub to keep it small will quickly result in a weak plant vulnerable to pests and diseases.

As a guideline for gardens where space is limited, even the largest 'backbone' shrubs should have a maximum height, whether potential or prunable, of 2.4m (8ft). A shrub of this height creates screening at and slightly above eye level, and provides a pleasant sense of enclosure without losing too much light or creating a feeling of being 'trapped'.

Certain shrubs, such as rue, fuchsia and Russian sage (*Perovskia atriplicifolia*), die back to ground level in hard winters, like herbaceous perennials, or are so straggly at the end of winter that they need cutting back severely to encourage attractive new growth. While these plants have much to commend them during the summer months, don't rely on them for a 'shrubby' year-round presence in the garden.

Shape and spread

The spread of a shrub is as important as its height, especially in a very small garden. Choose shrubs which have a diameter of less than 2.4m (8ft), and even smaller in tiny gardens. A wide-spreading shrub can smother weaker, nearby plants with its rampant growth. Some shrubs, such as fatsia, however, may have wide-spreading top growth which springs from sparse, narrow and largely upright stems, so shade-loving ground-cover plants can flourish under its canopy. Other shrubs, such as cinquefoil (*Potentilla*), appear thick and dense at ground level, with no room for underplanting.

If space is short, it is tempting to choose only rigidly upright shrubs. However, a balanced contrast of shapes, such as an upright rosemary grown near a dome-shaped senecio and low mounds of cotton lavender, is considerably more effective.

Choosing flowering shrubs

Although catalogues tend to illustrate shrubs in flower, remember that shrubs spend more of the year displaying berries and foliage. However, if flowers are what you want, some, such as lavender, are long-lasting and continue for weeks. Others, such as rock rose (*Cistus*) have short-lived flowers, but these are freely produced over many weeks.

▲ **Firethorn** *Pyracantha coccinea* is ideal for small gardens as its takes up little space and responds well to pruning. The creamy-white flowers in summer and red, orange or yellow berries in autumn are annual highlights.

▶ **Seaside shrubs** The New Zealand hebes object to hard frosts, but are tolerant of salt-laden sea sprays. 'Great Orme' is a compact shrub with narrow, evergreen leaves and tapering pink flowers.

▼ **Scarlet and white** The acid-loving, evergreen *Pieris formosa* creates its own colour combinations in late spring. The young scarlet leaves are enhanced by older, glossy-green foliage and white bell flowers.

Also consider whether the leaves are evergreen or deciduous – a good rule of thumb is to have evergreen plants composing 50% of the garden, to see it through autumn, winter and early spring. (An all-evergreen garden can be sombre; one devoid of evergreens is bare for much of the year.)

If the garden has enough colour and interest from annuals and perennials in summer, choose shrubs that come into their own when the summer display is over. For example, Japanese quince (*Chaenomeles speciosa*) has bright white, pink or red spring flowers, yellow fruits in autumn and an irregular, 'oriental' growth habit seen at its best in the winter months. Equally, the colourful stems of the red-barked dogwood (*Cornus alba* 'Sibirica') provide winter interest when leafless.

▶ **Blue grass** Outstanding among ornamental grasses, arching clumps of blue-green *Festuca glauca* add charm to any garden. Blue bell flowers emphasize the colour scheme.

▼ **Silver foliage** The centrepiece in this formal bed is a standard-trained *Artemisia arborescens*. It rises nobly from a bed of scarlet petunias rimmed with *Senecio maritimus* 'Dwarf Silver'.

Winter flowers are often more striking in the garden than summer species, simply because of their rarity value. A single camellia bush in flower is worth dozens of bedding plants, especially if it is visible from the living room.

Coloured foliage

Both evergreen and deciduous shrubs have leaves in a variety of colours, ranging from silvery-white and grey (cotton lavender, or *Santolina*) to creamy yellow and deep gold (*Choisya ternata* 'Sundance'), and even red-purple (*Berberis thunbergii* 'Atropurpurea').

Grey and silver plants are both attractive and easily available. There is a huge range of grey-leaved shrubs: artemisias, lavenders, santolinas, senecios, helichrysums, sun roses, rock roses, hebes, potentillas and willows among them. There are also grey-leaved varieties of familiar plants such as grey-leaved heather (*Calluna vulgaris* 'Silver Queen') and grey-leaved *Rosa rubrifolia*.

Of the trees, weeping silver pear (*Pyrus salicifolia* 'Pendula') is the most popular, and the most sensible choice for small gardens. For large gardens there are eucalyptus, white willows, especially *Salix alba* 'Sericea', and several white poplars.

Popular perennials include lamb's tongue (*Stachys lanata*), *Achillea taygetea* 'Moonshine', pearl everlastings, *Festuca glauca* and *Hosta sieboldiana*. Sea hollies (*Eryngium*), anthemis, globe thistle, *Veronica incana*, cardoon and globe artichoke are other options.

▲ **Blood-leaf** The aptly named *Iresine herbstii* is a shrubby perennial which is evergreen in frost-free areas. Its blood-red, prominently veined leaves on bright red stems benefit from the calming influence of the trailing, silver-grey stems of helichrysum.

▶ **Silver carpet** As ground-cover, the silver-leaved *Tanacetum haradjanii* offers dramatic contrast to darker foliage plants, such as the ornamental, woolly-leaved sage (*Salvia argentea*).

Grey-leaved biennials and annuals include mulleins (*Verbascum*), giant thistles (*Onopordum*), horned poppies and silver-leaved cineraria (*Senecio maritimus*). There are grey-leaved rockery pinks, saxifrages, sedums, androsaces, antennarias and sempervivums, and dwarf forms of achillea, artemisia, chrysanthemum and helichrysum which are ideal for delicate grey foliage at the front of borders.

Using grey-leaved plants

Grey-leaved foliage varies enormously in size, shape and texture. There are smooth and even fleshy grey-leaved plants – succulent houseleeks and stonecrops, for example. There are grey-leaved plants that look like lace, such as *Tanacetum densum* 'Amani', and some with enormous leaves, such as giant thistles and mulleins.

Grey-leaved plants are excellent for soothing and cooling down hot colours – fiery oranges, pinks, reds and purples. Grey is especially good with late summer and autumnal flowers such as dahlias, cosmos, zinnias and hollyhocks. It is equally effective in cooling down the 'hot' foliage colours of purple *Cotinus coggygria*, purple barberry and the fiery autumn red of stag's-horn sumach foliage.

Most pale grey-, white- and

▲ **Foliage displays** Variegated *Euonymus fortunei*, glossy green mahonia, silvery senecio and purple berberis provide year-round colour.

▼ **Garland flower** The prostrate *Daphne cneorum*, sweet-scented and rose-pink, flowers with the brooms.

silver-leaved plants automatically attract the eye. (The darker blue-leaved rue and *Hosta sieboldiana* are less prominent.) Being automatic focal points, such plants need very careful siting, and dotting them around a garden often results in a discordant, disjointed effect. Grey-leaved plants show up best against a dark background, such as a conifer hedge or a brick wall.

In grey and silver beds, or grey areas in a mixed bed, try to include several different plants, for added variety. A bed composed entirely of silvery, filigree foliage is liable to appear flat, especially in dull weather. But a bed containing round, filigree and sword-shaped foliage in a range of silvers, greys, whites and blues, and in a variety of textures and plant heights, is inevitably rich in both depth and detail.

Grey-leaved plants need light soil that is not too fertile, otherwise the leaves grow lush and green. They also need direct sunlight. Their silver, grey, white or blue colour is a protective measure to reduce transpiration in wind and hot summer sun, while shade has the opposite effect, encouraging lush, green growth. They also grow lanky in shade, in their search for light.

CLIMBING COMPANY

Even in a limited space, climbers – woody, herbaceous, perennial or annual – can make stunning associations with other climbers and shrubs of different habits.

Climbers add an extra dimension to a garden and are very useful in smaller gardens where space is limited. They can partner one another, create a beautiful mask for undistinguished or ugly walls and fences, enhance pergolas and arches or climb poles in a mixed border.

True climbers, mainly shrubby types but also some herbaceous species, are characterized by having weak, lax stems that need support to keep them upright. Some climbers, such as ivies and ornamental vines are self-clinging; others, like clematis and sweet peas, are equipped with tendrils which attach themselves to any available support. Yet others, such as climbing and rambling roses and winter jasmine, cannot support themselves and therefore must be tied into place.

Climbing plants have many roles in the garden. As well as hiding eyesores and complementing existing features, they can add beauty to old fruit trees – allow clematis and roses to scramble through their branches – and bring life to daunting north-facing sites. Ivies, climbing hydrangeas, the purple-flowered *Akebia quinata* and all *Parthenocissus* species thrive and flourish in such shady positions.

Climbers grow at different rates and should be in proportion to their supports. Wisteria easily grows to a spread of 15m (50ft) when well established, and the twice-yearly pruning operations to encourage the production of flowering shoots can be a daunting task. Where wall space is limited, *Jasminum nudiflorum* or sweet-

▶ **Pure passion** The passion flower (*Passiflora caerulea*) is an ideal focal point. It is so dramatic in colouring and form that it would clash with another climber. The large, white flowers with purple and yellow-stained centres open in summer on plants that climb rapidly in sheltered gardens. Grow shrubs around the base to provide colour from late winter onwards: evergreen, purple-flowered *Daphne odora* 'Aureomarginata' with white-margined leaves, and *Potentilla* × 'Elizabeth' whose yellow flowers bloom from late spring to early autumn.

▲ **Exuberant scrambler** If clematis is left to its own devices it will take support where it finds it, clambering up trees, twining around shrubs or scrambling among companions in mixed borders. The vivid colour of this large-flowered hybrid is softened by silver-grey artemisias.

▶ **Shades of pink** The exotic-looking *Actinidia kolomikta* is a vigorous climbing vine, with magnificent tri-coloured leaves of dark green, pink and white. It is accompanied by a tall-growing escallonia whose drooping racemes of deep pink, tubular flowers perfectly match the unusual leaf colours.

◀ **Wall companions** Given a large expanse of shady wall, the honeysuckle *Lonicera × tellmanniana* will quickly climb to a height of 4.5m (15ft) or more. Its spectacular clusters of glowing coppery-yellow flowers in high summer blend well with *Clematis* 'Mrs Cholmondely', whose soft blue flowers continue well into autumn when the leaves of the ornamental vine, *Vitis coignetiae*, begin to turn vivid crimson.

scented honeysuckle are much easier to control.

The ubiquitous Russian vine (*Polygonum baldschuanicum*) is immensely vigorous. It is a popular choice because of its capacity to smother everything in its path with clouds of creamy-white flowers. Plant it with discretion where it can tumble at will without interfering with other, more select plants.

Clematis, the queen of climbers, likes company. The large-flowered hybrids that adorn pillars, pergolas and walls associate well with climbing roses and green ivies, while the smaller-flowered species of clematis ramble naturally among trees and shrubs. The nodding purple bells of *C. viticella* look delightful with the flat heads of white or pink lace-cap hydrangeas or *Viburnum plicatum*. The scrambling *C. tangutica* with its superb combination of yellow lantern flowers and silky seed heads, looks even better when combined

with the tubular orange blooms of climbing Chilean glory flower (*Eccremocarpus scaber*).

Ivies are sympathetic partners. Few plants can rival the variegated *Hedera helix* 'Goldheart' ('Jubilee') for brightening up a wall. It has small, green leaves splashed with yellow that never fades and which gleams in shade. It is perfect for clothing a wall when mixed with *Tropaeolum speciosum* for bright scarlet summer colour. Another variegated ivy, *Hedera colchica* 'Dentata Variegata' is notably vigorous, easily covering a wall 6-9m (20-30ft) high, and bearing the largest leaves of all ivies, edged with a broad margin of creamy-yellow.

Herbaceous climbers

Several annuals, in addition to sweet peas, make rapid growth and are ideal for summer screens. They will grow on their own along wire mesh or pillar supports, or against ivy-covered walls. The cup

and saucer plant (*Cobaea scandens*) grows to 3.6m (12ft) and produces large, bell-shaped flowers which change from green to purple by late summer. Morning-glory (*Ipomoea tricolor*) reaches 2.4m (8ft) in a sunny spot and bears blue trumpet flowers which open every morning.

Perennial climbers include the everlasting pea (*Lathyrus latifolius*), which grows up to 3m (10ft) tall and bears rose-purple flowers that mix well with yellow day lilies and blue *Salvia × superba*. The golden hop (*Humulus lupulus* 'Aureus') can reach 6m (20ft) in a season and is ideal for training up pergolas together with large-flowered clematis hybrids.

▼ **Clematis clones** Large-flowered clematis hybrids, such as the petunia-red 'Ernest Markham' and violet 'Mrs N. Thompson', make a glorious show grouped with the dainty yellow flower lanterns and silvery seed heads of *Clematis tangutica*.

◄ **Arched profusion** Pink and scarlet sweet peas (*Lathyrus odoratus*) scramble through ripening marrows trained up a metal pergola. Massive sunflowers nod from above, as if recognizing other members of the daisy family — golden rudbeckias which line the path.

▶ **Tree climber** The rampant *Clematis montana* is festooned in late spring with a mass of starry white flowers. It grows happily on a north-facing wall and will clamber through tall trees. Here, its flowers mingle with the yellow drapes of *Laburnum* × *watereri*.

▼ **Autumn glory** The self-clinging Boston ivy (*Parthenocissus tricuspidata*) is a familiar sight on house walls. It is a source of delight when the leaves turn crimson and scarlet before falling in autumn. The cream-edged leaves of its evergreen partner, the Canary Island ivy (*Hedera canariensis* 'Variegata'), provides fine contrast.

59

▲ **Accommodating ivy** The common ivy (*Hedera helix*) grows as ground-cover or wall covering in the most inhospitable places. Golden varieties like 'Buttercup' add splashes of light to dull sites and make excellent support for clematis, such as *C. montana* 'Rubens'.

▶ **Pillar climbers** Choose climbers of moderate vigour for low pergolas and pillars, otherwise the floral display will be above eye-level. Clematis and honeysuckle make good partners and can be kept within bounds with annual pruning.

▼ **Nelly Moser** One of the most popular clematis, 'Nelly Moser', flowers twice — in early and late summer. A young specimen associates well with nicotianas.

► **Sweet welcome** Roses and clematis make classic partnerships. Here, 'New Dawn' rose climbs up to meet blue *Clematis* 'Jackmanii Superba' to create a delightful summer framework.

61

◄ **Sweet peas** The ever-popular sweet peas (*Lathyrus odoratus*) flower from early summer to early autumn on plants that grow up to 3m (10ft) high with adequate support. Sweet peas can be cordon-trained, but they look more appealing at the rear of borders where their flowers create a colourful tapestry for other plants. Sweet peas are available in mixed and single colours, and provide an unending supply of cut flowers if regularly dead-headed.

This multi-coloured group is appropriately fronted by pastel shades — pale lemon lady's mantle (*Alchemilla mollis*) and dwarf blue and white *Convolvulus tricolor*.

▼ **Morning glory** The common morning glory (*Ipomoea purpurea*) is a half-hardy annual, but in its brief growing season it will climb to a height of 3m (10ft) if sited against a sunny fence. Here, its mass of purple trumpet flowers are exquisitely partnered by another annual climber, the yellow-flowered canary creeper (*Tropaeolum peregrinum*), a relation of the common nasturtium. It reaches much the same height as the morning glory and provides brilliant contrast in flower shape and colour.

◄ **Flame creeper** Another relation of nasturtium, the scarlet flame creeper (*Tropaeolum speciosum*) is a hardy perennial climber. It thrives in acid soil with its roots in shade and its flowers in sun. Good companions include ivies, spring-flowering *Bergenia* 'Silberlicht' and *Gentiana asclepiadea* which bears deep blue flowers in summer.

ROSES LIKE COMPANY

**Roses are frequently condemned to solitary
confinement – grown in beds on their own and surrounded
by bare earth. But roses look more attractive in mixed beds,
against a background of complementary
flowers and foliage.**

There are roses for every garden and almost any garden position. Some, like the old-fashioned shrub roses, have one short though exquisitely fragrant flowering season in early summer, which is followed by brightly coloured hips in autumn. Others, notably modern bush roses and climbers, are in bloom almost continuously from early summer until the autumn frosts.

The rose is widely acclaimed as the 'flower of all flowers'. It is worth taking time to consider its position in the garden – some are so splendid in bloom and in form that they deserve to be grown as specimen shrubs. Others, like bush roses, look stunning partnered by their own kind, while shrub roses are set off to perfection in mixed borders in the company of well-chosen perennials and shrubs.

The growth pattern of roses is as diverse as their form – there are roses that hug the ground, rooting and spreading as they grow; others that fit neatly into rock garden pockets or clamber 10m (30ft) or more up tall trees and house walls; and yet others that lace their prickly branches so closely together that they form a dense barrier hedge.

Traditional layouts

Roses are set in a strict pattern in formal beds. Bush roses (hybrid tea roses and floribundas) grow well under these conditions as they do not have to compete with other permanent plants for soil moisture and nutrients. Sited in an island bed, they will benefit from good light and air circulation and are also much easier to manage in terms of pruning, mulching and dead-heading. Additionally, their massed blooming in formal beds has more impact than if they are grown singly.

Hybrid tea roses and floribundas do not mix well, mainly because the cluster-flowered floribundas are more vigorous and spreading. Grow them in separate beds, and for the most pleasing results, stick to types that harmonize both in habit and colour.

One drawback with rose beds is the amount of bare soil that is visible. Underplanting with low-growing bedding plants can overcome this problem – try alyssum or lobelias, compact ageratums, dwarf marigolds and busy Lizzies. Traditional rose beds are frequently edged with low, primly pruned hedges of box or lavender. For winter interest, the bare ground can be occupied by snowdrops, miniature irises, or early crocuses.

▶ **Formal rose bed** A colour scheme of pink, blue and green is dominated by the large-flowered hybrid tea rose 'Madame Butterfly'. The shell-pink, yellow-flushed rose is grown in an island bed edged with clipped mounds of blue-grey rue (*Ruta graveolens* 'Jackman's Blue').

Blue bedding pansies (*Viola* × *wittrockiana*) cover the ground beneath the roses; with rigorous dead-heading they will provide colour from early spring through summer and into autumn.

▲ **'Spek's Yellow'** This large-flowered bush rose can be rather gawky in appearance, as its spindly stems are only sparsely clothed with foliage. It is best planted in a shrub border where low-growing foliage plants can conceal its base. Here, it rises like a bright yellow beacon above clumps of purple-leaved sage (*Salvia officinalis* 'Purpurascens').

▲ **'Constance Spry'** The large, fully double flowers of this vigorous shrub rose are clear pink and heavily scented. They are borne in early and high summer and associate well with the hardy geraniums such as *Geranium pratense* 'Johnson's Blue', valued for its dark green, deeply cut leaves and clear blue flowers.

◀ **'Queen Elizabeth'** This well-known floribunda rose forms a tall and stiff bush, 1.8m (6ft) or more in height. It bears most of its sweet-scented flowers at the crown. Their deep pink colour is displayed to perfection against a backdrop of dark conifers. The leggy stems can be shrouded by a suitable foreground — here, 90cm (3ft) high, blue-flowered rosemary (*Rosmarinus officinalis*) is joined by clumps of lower-growing lavender (*Lavandula angustifolia* 'Hidcote').

Roses in borders

Shrub roses formed the large rose shrubberies of bygone days, but they can look equally good incorporated in small shrub or mixed borders. They have many advantages over bedding roses – they require only light pruning, for instance – and are comparable with the best flowering shrubs. Like other shrubs, modern and old-fashioned shrub roses give maximum impact when planted in groups of at least three.

In mixed borders intermingle shrub roses with perennials which have striking foliage as well as attractive flowers. Lady's mantle, for example, is excellent for

camouflaging the unsightly stems of some shrub roses. Silvery plants and evergreens look particularly attractive with roses, either as an edging at the front of the border or as interplanting. Both provide interest over a long period – silver foliage during summer and evergreens all year round.

Glorious effects can be achieved with a background planting of delphiniums. Their elegant blue spires look particularly effective with pink, white and red shrub roses. For a more restrained effect, try the plume poppy (*Macleaya cordata*) with its green-silver leaves and delicate pink-buff flowers. This plant produces a

subtle effect when grown behind a creamy-orange rose such as 'Buff Beauty': a long-lasting combination that will delight throughout the summer.

Old-fashioned roses often flower only once a year – usually in early to mid-summer. For the most spectacular effect, choose partners which bloom at the same time as the roses but keep their flowers longer to divert attention from the roses' fading beauty.

For old-style roses with attractive foliage and colourful hips, consider *Rosa moyesii*, *R. glauca* and *R.* × 'Canary Bird'. Rugosa hybrid roses which do double duty as hedging plants, are real gems in the shrub border. Generally around 1.5m (5ft) high, they are outstanding for their rich green, heavily veined foliage, and for their heady fragrance. The pink 'Fru Dagmar Hastrup' and the crimson 'Scabrosa' bear large decorative hips among the last of the flower crop. 'Roseraie de l'Hay', considered the finest rugosa rose, deserves a place in any shrub border.

Old-fashioned rose blooms are often much flatter and rounder than the newer bush roses (hybrid tea and floribunda). This flower form – and the soft colours associated with old roses – can be pleasantly enhanced by a closely planted mixture of contrasting flower forms. Try columbines in shades of red, blue, pink and purple, the tall spikes of delphiniums or foxgloves, blue and white *Campanula persicifolia* and, later in the year, delicate pink or white Japanese anemones.

To complement the pretty flower form of old shrub roses, try planting double peonies, crane's-bills such as *Geranium* 'Johnson's Blue' and scented pinks, which will all add to the cottage garden effect.

Effective long-flowering shrubs for associating with old-style roses include lavender and *Potentilla fruticosa*, or any of the hardier sun roses (*Cistus* species).

Grey and silver-leaved plants such as artemisia, cotton lavender

◄ **Old-fashioned roses** The long arching stems of the Gallica rose, *Rosa* 'Complicata', are laden with large, bright pink flowers in early summer. The colour tones effectively with the tubular blooms of another old-fashioned charmer, tall-growing foxgloves.

65

▼ **Red and white companions** The elegant species rose, *Rosa moyesii*, is a firm favourite as a specimen shrub, growing up to 3m (10ft) tall. Its blood-red flowers borne in early summer, glow against creamy-white spikes of the evergreen Portugal laurel (*Prunus lusitanica*). At ground level, fans of *Cotoneaster horizontalis* are massed with minute leaves and small pink flowers.

▲ **First rose of summer** The arching and bristly stems of *Rosa* 'Cantabrigiensis' form the centrepiece in this early summer scene. The shrub is endowed with dainty, fern-like foliage and blooms of the softest yellow. Here, it towers above deep blue Belladonna delphiniums and sprawling clumps of white and pale purple sweet rocket (*Hesperis matronalis*).

▼ **Hybrid musk roses** Popular for their heady fragrance and long flowering season, musk roses like 'Penelope' are of vigorous arching habit. The enormous flower trusses are deep pink in the bud, open to pale pink and fade to creamy-white, forming an excellent backdrop for the steel-blue flower heads of the globe thistle (*Echinops ritro*).

At the foot of the group, the bright magenta blooms and silvery foliage of campion (*Lychnis coronaria*) complete the colour composition.

▲ **Modern shrub rose** Resembling apple blossom, 'Ballerina' bears large sprays of pale pink, white-eyed flowers in summer and autumn. Rarely exceeding 1.2m (4ft) in height and spread, this dainty shrub is at home in a mixed border. Here, its delicate colours are complemented by the grey-green foliage and lavender-blue flowers of catmint (*Nepeta* × *faassenii*).

▼ **Mixing old and new** The splendid Rugosa rose 'Roseraie de l'Hay' flowers almost continuously from early summer to autumn. Its tall branches set with crimson-purple flowers make a rich background for the modern shrub rose 'Erfurt'. This, too, is deliciously scented, carmine-red and creamy-eyed. Double-flowered peonies add to a symphony of red and pink which, on the left, includes *Rosa* 'Complicata'.

◀ **Bourbon roses** Typified by their large bowl-shaped blooms and intense fragrance, Bourbon roses flower from early summer until the autumn frosts. 'Mme Isaac Pereire' bears distinctive deep pink, quartered flowers and is a large shrub which is ideal for background planting.

Clumps of *Geranium endressii* flower simultaneously with the roses and make worthy companions with their deeply divided leaves and clear pink blooms.

▶ **Pillar rose** Left to its own devices and tied loosely to a tall, strong stake, the Hybrid Musk rose 'Buff Beauty' will arch its 1.8m (6ft) tall branches like a fountain. The sweetly-scented flowers are creamy-yellow darkening to apricot and are carried in great profusion in early and mid-summer, with a second display in early autumn.

Such soft colours demand companions that will not detract from the shrub's beauty in bloom. Here, it rises in summer from a sea of blue-flowered catmint (*Nepeta × faassenii*) pierced with black-eyed white poppies (*Papaver orientale* 'Perry's White) and golden and red-brown bearded *Iris* 'Staten Island'.

▼ Miniature roses The delicacy of miniature roses is easily overwhelmed, but here the airy grace of blue *Campanula cochlearifolia* enhances the elegant 'Perla de Monserrat', which is exceptionally compact, even for a miniature rose, at about 23cm (9in) high.

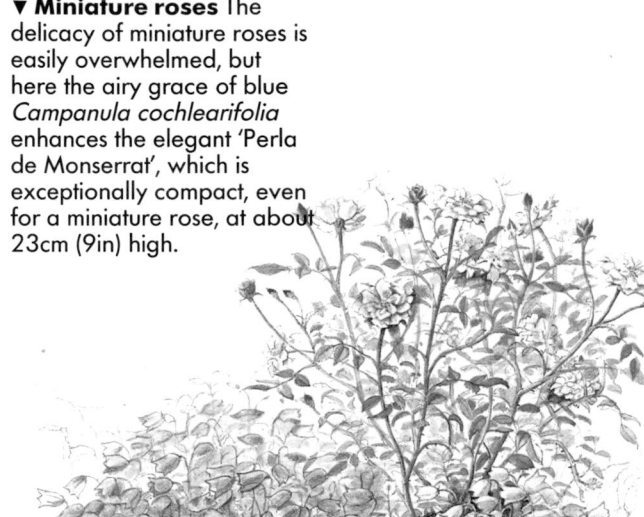

▲ Traditional partnership A tumbling profusion of climbing and rambling roses forms the perfect background for tall perennials such as delphiniums. Vigorous rambling roses such as 'Wedding Day', seen here trailing over a wall, are ideal for growing up trees. The large clusters of lemon-white flowers are sweetly scented.

◄ Old favourites The vigorous 'Albertine' is one of the most popular of the rambling roses. It is clothed with a mass of richly scented, double coppery-pink flowers in early summer. Although brief, the display is continued for several more weeks as the Rugosa rose 'Scabrosa' unfolds its large, single crimson-purple flowers.

Excellent for clothing fences and walls — and the rugosas for hedging as well — the base of the roses are hidden by a tumbling planting of red valerians (*Centranthus ruber*) and white feverfews (*Chrysanthemum parthenium*).

◄ **Yellow and blue symphony** The hybrid species rose 'Harison's Yellow' is an easy-going shrub up to 1.8m (6ft) tall, which is resplendent in early summer with large, semi-double flowers of clear yellow. As the rose begins to fade, its companion, the Chilean potato vine (*Solanum crispum*), comes into bloom, producing large clusters of yellow-eyed purple-blue flowers well into late summer and autumn.

▼ **Golden showers** Subtle colour combinations can be as effective as strong contrasts. This partnership between yellow climbing roses and the strong-growing honeysuckle (*Lonicera* × *tellmanniana*), with its coppery-yellow flowers, is soothing to the eye and is particularly restful on hot summer days. The group displays subtle differences in leaf texture and flower colour and density. Climbing yellow roses for similar associations include 'Dreaming Spires', 'Golden Showers', 'Mermaid' and 'Schoolgirl'.

(*Santolina chamaecyparissus*) and *Stachys lanata* make a soft carpet around the base of thorny stems and complement the soft shades of old-fashioned roses.

Other good foliage partners include the evergreen purple-leaved sage (*Salvia officinalis* 'Purpurascens'), soft-textured *Alchemilla mollis*, bold hostas and sprawling greyish green catmint (*Nepeta* × *faassenii*).

For a striking contrast to the mounded form of many shrub roses, use the distinctive sword-like foliage of irises or the smaller *Sisyrinchium striatum*, whose creamy flowers complement yellow or white roses.

Standards and miniatures
Standard roses are hybrid teas or floribundas grafted on to tall, bare stems of dog or rugosa roses. Weeping standards are rambling roses budded on to a standard stem. They are mainly used as dot

plants to give height to beds and free-standing borders of bush roses, annuals and low-growing perennials. They can also be grown on their own as specimen plants.

They look particularly spectacular in beds flanking a drive or broad path, the ground beneath occupied by annuals, compact perennials, silver-leaved foliage plants or dwarf forms of lavender.

Miniature and patio roses, dainty replicas of their hybrid tea and floribunda relations, are at the other end of the scale. On average 30-45cm (1-1½ft) high, they come in all the usual rose shades and as bicoloureds, too. Although they can be used to edge beds and borders, their charm is more obvious if they are sited at eye level – in raised beds, rock garden pockets and window boxes. Plant them in groups for greater impact – the effect of a single plant is often rather lost.

Rose hedges
Many roses are particularly suitable for hedging and barriers, the best being the shrubby types – they need little if any pruning, and their strong stems can be allowed to interlace. Like other deciduous hedging plants, they lose their leaves in winter but still form effective wind filters, and most of them flower throughout the summer months.

For barrier hedges, few can rival the rugosa hybrid roses when given some support – prickly stems will keep all intruders at a distance. Some, such as 'Blanc Double de Courbert' and 'Roseraie de l'Hay', form dense thickets up to 2.4m (8ft) high.

▼ **Rose garden** There are no limits to the true rosarians passion for roses. Climbers and ramblers, shrubs and bushes display variations in the shape, colour and texture of the incomparable rose.

For a medium-sized hedge, 1.2-1.8m (4-6ft) high, choose between another fragrant musk rose, the silver-pink 'Felicia' and rugosa hybrid roses such as 'Rubra', the white single 'Alba' or the semi-double 'Schneezwerg'.

Interior or edging hedges, dividing one part of the garden from another, should be kept comparatively low. Use small, repeat-flowering shrub roses, such as the elegant pink 'Angelina' and the red, white-eyed 'Marjorie Fair' which do not grow much above 90cm (3ft). Alternative choices include the pale pink Centifolia 'Rose de Meaux' and the rose-pink Gallica rose 'Empress Josephine', although they flower only once in the season.

Hybrid teas and floribundas, with their erect growth, are not reliably wind-resistant on exposed sites, and they need severe annual pruning if they are to flower abundantly. The popular floribunda 'Queen Elizabeth' is sometimes used as a hedge – it is strong and vigorous – but, left as an unpruned hedging plant, it tends to grow leggy and flower less freely.

Climbing roses
Climbing roses are perfect for training on house walls and fences, pergolas, pillars and arches, rustic screens and tall

▲ **Prostrate roses** Some modern shrub roses, such as the 90cm (3ft) high 'Raubritter', have a sprawling habit that makes them ideal for covering banks. They are also useful in formal island beds where interplanting would break up the uniform scheme.

▼ **Weeping standards** Rambler roses grafted on to bare, 1.5-1.8cm (5-6ft) tall stems of *Rosa canina* and trained over an umbrella-shaped wire frame, trail elegantly to the ground. Rose standards make stunning focal points and should be viewed in isolation.

trees. By the nature of their growth, they need strong and sturdy support. Additionally, their shoots may need tying in regularly. Dead-head them frequently to keep them looking at their best.

Their performance (in terms of their vigour, hardiness, eventual height and flowering display) depends largely on their complex origins. Before choosing a climber for a particular situation, it is worth checking it against catalogues from various reputable rose growers.

Repeat-flowering sports bred from early hybrid tea roses are extremely vigorous climbers, and are particularly suitable for house walls. When well established, they average a height of 4.5m (15ft) and are often more spectacu-

▶ **Rose-clad arch** Richly scented repeat-flowering climbers of moderate vigour are ideal for romantic arbours, pillars and arches.

▼ **Miniature climber** Deprived of upright support, the climbing miniature rose 'Nozomi' forms a spreading ground-cover shrub, densely set with clusters of pearly pink blooms.

lar in bloom than their bushy relatives, especially the crimson 'Climbing Etoile de Hollande' and the soft pink 'Climbing Cécile Brunner'.

Modern repeat-flowering climbers average about 3m (10ft) in height and bear more or less continuous clusters of semi or fully double blooms. They are particularly ideal for growing up walls, pillars and rustic screens, and some varieties, such as 'Danse du Feu', 'Golden Showers', 'Mermaid' and 'New Dawn', are suitable for northerly sites.

Rambling roses are of exceptional vigour and reach their full potential only where they can be allowed to clamber unchecked up tall trees and similar structures. Most spectacular is *Rosa filipes* 'Kiftsgate' whose 10m (30ft) long stems are smothered in early summer with creamy-white, scented flowers. 'Bobbie James' is similar, but with larger blooms, while the apple-scented 'François Juranville' is a glowing pink colour. More moderate types, such as the ever popular 'Albertine' and 'Dorothy Perkins', will ramble happily over fences and hedges.

Rambler roses flower only once,

usually in early summer; they should be pruned immediately after flowering – the old flowered shoots being cut back and young replacement shoots tied in.

Combining climbing roses and clematis is a traditional way of having double colour on wall space. Honeysuckles can also intermingle with large climbing roses or ramblers for rich scents.

Ground-cover roses

Most so-called ground-cover roses are really wide-spreading shrub roses whose lower branches hug the ground and smother weeds. They look pretty tumbling over low retaining walls or covering tree stumps.

The recently introduced 'County' roses flower continuously from early summer until autumn on plants about 30cm (1ft) high. The 'Gamebird' roses are truly prostrate, spreading a carpet up to 3m (10ft) wide, studded with small scented blooms in mid to late summer – pale pink in 'Grouse', pure white in 'Partridge' and rosy-pink in 'Pheasant'.

The rambling *Rosa wichuraiana* is naturally prostrate and will spread widely if allowed to

▲ **Patio roses** Miniature bush roses are ideal for growing in pots, window boxes and sink gardens. They flower almost continuously through the summer if regularly dead-headed and fed.

trail along the ground; so, too, will the thorny, white-flowered *Rosa × paulii*. Both are suitable for semi-wild gardens or for covering large banks.

Specimen roses

Old garden roses are perfect for use as specimen plants, as are weeping standards trained on metal frames. However, there are no hard and fast rules for which species to choose, although one which flowers prolifically and over a long period will be more rewarding. One rose lover will enthuse over the golden and copper-red *Rosa foetida bicolor*, another will swear by *Rosa moyesii*, whose glistening scarlet flowers are followed by clusters of red, bottle-shaped hips. No flower arranger would willingly give up the purple-grey foliage of *Rosa rubrifolia*, while the rippling sprays of ferny leaves and golden flowers on 'Canary Bird' are delightful.

Roses in containers

Even the smallest garden or paved basement can have a display of roses. Several dwarf floribundas and miniature roses are neat and compact enough to grow in troughs, window boxes and other types of planters. They do require sun or dappled light though – no rose will thrive in dense shade. Like other container plants, they need frequent watering, perfect drainage and feeding with a proprietary liquid rose fertilizer at least once a month during the growing season.

A recently introduced group known as 'patio' roses are compact enough to be grown as pot plants. Most are repeat-flowering, with perfectly formed hybrid tea- and floribunda-shaped blooms.

Partners for rose hips

For many gardeners, the lovely simplicity of species roses is all too fleeting, but some of these shrubs come to the fore again in autumn, when their fruits appear in contrast to their handsome foliage.

Once the petals have fallen, the hips develop quickly, swelling into globular, bottle or flask shapes, while their skins ripen to gleaming shades of red, orange, maroon and purple-black.

These informal shrubs are best planted in mixed borders with other shrubs and plants chosen to enhance their late summer beauty.

Rosa rugosa, unlike many species roses, blooms continuously throughout summer. Its last flush of flowers – light pink in 'Fru Dagmar Hastrup', magenta in 'Scabrosa' and silky white in 'Alba' – mingles with the fat, round crimson hips. Its deeply veined leaves, turning yellow in autumn, would look handsome against the foliage of *Cotinus coggygria* 'Royal Purple', with Michaelmas daisies planted in front.

The early-summer, white or pink flowers of burnet rose (*R. pimpinellifolia*, syn. *R. spinosissima*) – a lowish suckering shrub – are followed by purplish black 2cm (¾in) wide hips, set amid dainty fern-like foliage. White-flowered

Viola cornuta 'Alba' would look effective weaving among its low-sweeping branches.

Many hip-bearing roses, such as *R. rubrifolia* and *R. moyesii*, are bare-stemmed at the base. To hide this unattractive feature, plant *Fuchsia magellanica* 'Versicolor',

grey artemisias or lavenders, and *Salvia officinalis* 'Purpurea' to the front. Additionally, *R. moyesii* could be partly hidden by *Aster × frikartii* 'Mönch', whose lavender-blue flowers begin in late summer, or by 90cm (3ft) tall, orange-red *Curtonus paniculatus*.

► **Autumn fruits** Outstanding in flower, foliage and fruit, deep red *Rosa moyesii* 'Geranium' droops glossy red, flask-shaped hips over a footing of *Vinca major* 'Variegata'.

► **Hip flasks** As summer merges into early autumn, the splendid *Rosa moyesii* puts on a second spectacular display. The single, glowing red flowers with golden centres are replaced by numerous fine, flask-shaped fruits that flare into orange-red and droop gracefully from the arching stems.

This vigorous 3m (10ft) high shrub rose with its elegant foliage, should be planted as a specimen shrub or in a large border where its stems can mingle with other plants, enhancing them first with flowers and secondly with hips. A Lawson cypress (*Chamaecyparis lawsoniana* 'Pembroke Blue'), for example, creates a misty blue-green foil for the fountain of prickly stems.

The strong vertical emphasis of such a partnership is tempered by the rounded shapes in a foreground planting of *Hydrangea macrophylla* 'Lanark White'.

▼ **Foliage contrasts** The species rose *Rosa glauca*, formerly known as *R. rubrifolia*, is chiefly grown for its handsome foliage, much prized by flower arrangers. Carried on violet-red stems, the graceful foliage has a bluish-grey sheen that blends attractively with the small red-purple flowers in early summer. In autumn, the shrub bears smallish red hips.

Such a dainty appearance demands the contrast of stronger foliage plants — bear's breeches (*Acanthus spinosus*) with its deep green, leathery and spiny leaves makes an admirable partner.

▲ **Autumn splendour** The Rugosa rose 'Fru Dagmar Hastrup' is ideal for small gardens. It is compact and grows at most 1.5m (5ft) high and wide; it needs little attention and thrives on sandy soil. The pink, sweetly scented flowers open in summer amid wrinkled dark green foliage.

Plump hips appear from late summer onwards, before the leaves take on clear yellow autumn colours. *Sedum* 'Autumn Joy' makes an attractive companion, its dense flat flower heads maturing through pale pink to deep russet-red.

Border companions

Bulbs, herbaceous perennials and half-hardy and hardy annuals and biennials display a kaleidoscope of flower colours from spring until late autumn. Such a profusion of colour needs careful handling or the effect can be discordant, one of clashing colours and badly contrasting flower shapes.

Hardy perennials, which start to grow in spring, flower in summer and die back in autumn before the renewal of their life cycle, were the traditional occupants of Edwardian borders. Today, they are more often found in mixed beds and borders where they can occupy either centre stage or play supporting roles among shrubs and foliage plants. They are at their best when framed by foliage so that they weave a tapestry of complementary colours.

Clever associations ensure that a colour scheme can be maintained for months. For example, the classic blue spires of delphiniums are glorious in early summer, and their place can be taken by clumps of tall bellflowers which continue the blue theme into early autumn. Annuals can serve the same purpose, filling gaps in borders and adding colour where early perennials have finished. They can be sown *in situ*, perhaps among low ground-cover, or grown in pots to be moved around for instant colour where it is needed.

Bulbs are invaluable in the garden. With only basic help from the gardener, they give a succession of colour from late winter through summer and into autumn. They take up little room and effectively partner all other garden plants, from tall trees to ground-hugging ivies. Bulbs flower throughout the changing seasons: daffodils, tulips and fritillaries in spring, irises and lilies in high summer, dahlias and nerines in autumn, and dainty cyclamen and snowdrops in winter.

Summer charm White regal lilies and pink mallow funnels (*Lavatera* 'Silver Cup') add a bright touch to a mixed border.

GARDEN BORDERS

With careful selection, hardy perennials can be grouped to form garden displays of long-lasting associations.

Herbaceous borders are an important part of the traditional English garden, giving magnificent colour displays lasting four or five months. They reached their zenith in Victorian and Edwardian gardens, examples of which can be seen at some stately homes.

Mixed borders developed more recently, mainly because of the need to find labour-saving ways of gardening. These contain a mixture of plant types and are especially popular in small gardens where they can provide year-round interest if plants are carefully selected. A typical mixed border will include a core of shrubs, with herbaceous and evergreen perennials, bulbs and bedding plants, and occasionally a small specimen tree. Mixed borders tend to be informal and

give a longer show than herbaceous borders, and they need less attention and maintenance.

Mixed or herbaceous borders

There are a few factors to take into account when considering whether to plant a mixed or herbaceous border – decide if the border should provide interest throughout the year, work out realistically how much time can be spared for maintenance, and study the size and type of site available.

Well-planted herbaceous borders provide spectacular displays of colour from spring to autumn, but tend to look dead and bare during the winter months. Mixed borders are unlikely to rival herbaceous borders at the height of the summer season, but with careful planning, the wider range of

▲ **Autumn partners** Hemp agrimony (*Eupatorium purpureum*) is one of the tallest of herbaceous plants reaching a height of 2.4m (7ft). Its clusters of purple-pink flowers on purple stems belong in large herbaceous borders or as an ideal partner for the blue-flowered *Hydrangea macrophylla*. Both flower in late summer and autumn.

▼ **Pink parfait** The French lavender (*Lavandula stoechas*) makes a pleasant change from the more commonly grown, blue English lavender. It flowers earlier, too, and bears purple-pink flower spikes with prominent purple bracts beneath the petals. The pink African daisy (*Dimorphotheca barberiae*) makes a perfect companion.

▶ Waterside association
The lush foliage of moisture-loving plants brings a look of well-established maturity to a streamside planting.

In late spring, the leafy rosettes of *Primula japonica* support 60cm (2ft) tall candelabras of pastel-coloured flowers. Alongside these, the magnificent white-edged, boldly ribbed leaves of *Hosta crispula* create an eye-catching centrepoint. Spreading clumps of fern-like astilbes, pale bronze as the leaves unfold, will later replace the faded primula blooms with their fluffy flower spires.

◀ Shades of gold The plantain lily (*Hosta fortunei* 'Albopicta') is lovely from the moment in spring when its tightly furled leaves open out and become clear yellow with a pale green edge. Later on the yellow pales and the green darkens until each leaf is patterned in two shades of green which take on golden tones with the onset of autumn frost. Such cool elegance in high summer blends perfectly with the gloriously golden Aurelian lily 'Golden Clarion'.

plants used can give year-round interest and colour.

Formal and informal borders

Formal borders are usually long, straight-edged rectangles with plants arranged in orderly schemes of specific colours and types, and of exact gradations – tall plants at the back, medium-sized in the centre and low-edging plants to the front. The neat and tidy effect adds to the geometry of the border.

Informal borders can be rectangular or curving, and contain less regimented planting. Groups of plants intermingle rather than being set out in distinct patterns which are repeated at regular intervals in order to give coherence to the formal scheme. Gradations are less obvious in informal borders, and plants are allowed to spill over the edges.

Colour schemes

Formal borders are arranged in orderly schemes of specific colour groups repeated at regular intervals. Informal borders contain plants in a range of colours. The planting may seem random, although it should be as carefully planned as in a formal border.

Variation in colour within one group of plants is more welcome in an informal border than in a formal one. The proportions of colours in an informal border tend to vary, with huge drifts of one shade punctuated by small splashes of contrasting colour. Many herbaceous perennials are best planted in groups of three or five depending on their eventual spread, although a few, such as bear's breeches (*Acanthus mollis*), like most shrubs, are large and imposing enough to be planted as individual specimens.

In general, taller plants are usually planted at the back of a border which is backed by a fence, wall or hedge, with shorter plants in front to create a tiered effect. Variety and informality can be introduced by bringing forward one or two clumps or individual plants of medium height. This is especially sensible with mid- and late-season plants which can then hide the gaps left by earlier-flowering types. The tallest plants should be placed in the centre of free-standing borders.

▼ **Summer profusion** Informal drifts of herbaceous perennials, predominantly in shades of pink and red, are held together with scattered stands of spiky, metallic-blue hollies (*Eryngium maritimum*). A background of conifers and a raised urn bright with summer bedding raise the view from the horizontal perspective.

▲ **Autumn colours** The fleshy-leaved *Sedum spectabile* is one of the joys of autumn as its large, flattened flower heads gradually deepen to richer shades. Here, a carmine-pink form, 'Carmen', nestles near tall-stemmed blue *Agapanthus* hybrids. The two are complemented by a band of silvery *Artemisia ludoviciana*. In the background, Michaelmas daisies (*Aster novae-angliae* 'Harrington's Pink') add yet more autumn colour.

◄ **Butterfly plants** The autumn-flowering sedums (see above) are adored by butterflies, but one plant above all others attracts these charming insects in late summer. The grey-leaved *Buddleia fallowiana* 'Lochinch' with its violet-blue flower spikes, plays generous host to swarms of butterflies. In a small garden, make a feature of the shrub in a mixed border, matching it with pink-flowered tree mallow (*Lavatera olbia*) and the cerise-pink trumpet flowers of *Crinum × powellii*.

▶ **Colour spots** Bright highlights can be introduced to herbaceous borders with temporary plants. In summer, many borders lack colour after the first, early-summer flush and before later-flowering perennials come into bloom. Here, a miniature, fancy-leaved, salmon-pink pelargonium lights up a corner where the cone flowers of sea hollies (*Eryngium maritimum*) have yet to develop their blue colour.

The lime-green flower sprays of lady's mantle (*Alchemilla mollis*) cascade to one side; at the other, a golden-leaved spiraea is thrown into clear relief by a pot plant.

▼ **Focal points** Use pot plants for impact where, for example, paving gives way to grass or where lifted spring bulbs have left bare patches in a bed. A group of potted plants has a far greater visual effect than plants which are dotted about individually. A group can be extended to when flower colour is lacking or when contrast in shape or form is required.

Daily watering of pot plants is essential, as is regular dead-heading to maintain continuous flowering. At the end of summer, move half-hardy types to a frost-free greenhouse and keep them almost dry during winter.

Focal points

Any border, formal or informal, can be planned around one or more focal points. Provide emphasis with bold foliage, such as yuccas or castor-oil plants (*Ricinus*), and include clumps of the invaluable hostas or similar foliage plants near the front. Silver and grey leaves have a calming influence and are useful for separating one colour group from another.

Aim for pleasing colour combinations that will continue throughout the flowering season. Include perennials, bulbs and shrubs that will provide autumn and winter colour as well. Simple mixtures, such as blue, pink and white, provide a wide choice of flowering plants. Other schemes could be based on blues, yellows and creams – for a 'hotter' effect replace the blues with orange, reds

83

▲ **Foliage partners** The Chinese plantain lily (*Hosta plantaginea*) with its long-stemmed, glossy green leaves, is a distinctive and beautiful foliage plant. Unlike other hostas, it needs a sunny spot where it can develop its tall spikes of pure white trumpet flowers in late summer and early autumn. Here, it supplies magnificent contrast for the small, dark purple leaves of the smoke tree (*Cotinus coggygria* 'Royal Purple').

◄ **Leaf contrasts** Hostas are given plenty of room to show off their impressive leaves in the rich, moisture-retentive soil alongside a pool and in the light shade cast by a flowering crab apple tree. Contrasting in shape, size and colour, their differences are made even more apparent by young ferns pushing up their feathery fronds.

and purples mixed with grey-leaved foliage plants. Use varying leaf tints for contrast with cool hot colours and to act as accent points.

Single-colour schemes can be very beautiful – the white borders at Sissinghurst in Kent are justly famous – but they are much too limiting for small gardens. Successful one-colour borders rely totally on foliage, touches of subtle colour and a range of tones to break up what could otherwise be an amorphous mass of uninspiring colour.

Borders with a difference
Raised borders can rationalize natural level changes in a garden, or they could be created as a design feature – perhaps in a flat, town garden. They are much easier to maintain than long borders and have drier root con-

ditions, ideal for many alpines and hardy succulents. Such beds and borders could be used for single-colour schemes, or they could be devoted to plants of a single genus, such as irises, fuchsias or roses, or to a particular type of plant, such as culinary herbs or ferns.

Narrow or ribbon borders and beds planted with parallel rows of colourful annuals interspersed with bulbs for added height are ideal for lining paths. Single colour schemes can look effective in such narrow beds, especially if planted in white, blue and pink, or silver and grey.

Seasonal groups
In a spacious garden, you can create a different border for each season of the year. Another alternative is to refurbish a herbaceous border several times a year by lift-

▲ **White for contrast** White flowers introduce an aura of calm and freshness to a herbaceous border; they also serve to accentuate other colours and give definition to a planting scheme. The focal point of this association is a trough of white single-flowered petunias topped by white chrysanthemums, with trailing yellow coreopsis at their feet.

ing plants after they have finished flowering, moving them to a reserve bed and then replacing them with varieties which come into flower later in the season.

However, this option is both labour- and time-consuming. Furthermore, most gardens have no space for reserve beds, so it is better to enjoy a spring and summer border and try to extend the display as far as possible into autumn and early winter.

It is sensible to include ever-green shrubs, perennials and other plants that hold interest outside the summer months. Early chrysanthemums, dahlias, asters, schizostylis, gladiolus, autumn-flowering crocus and colchicums, cyclamens and lilies can add colour to the garden until the first autumn frost.

Hellebores, winter-flowering iris, pulmonarias, aconites, camellias and viburnums sustain colour through to spring, when doronicums, bergenias, dicentras, primroses and lenten roses lead into early summer.

Bulbs are valuable for non-summer colour – small pockets of bare soil can be planted with crocus, snowdrops, winter aconites and anemones. Mark bare spaces and plant the bulbs as early in autumn as possible. Annuals, biennials and pot plants can be added for instant colour in early summer.

Border maintenance

Herbaceous borders are more permanent than bedding schemes, but they still need periodic renovation. Except for perennials such as acanthus and peonies which resent root disturbance, most plants benefit from being lifted and divided every three or five years, and some, such as the Michaelmas daisies, deteriorate in shape, size

▲ **Lady's mantle** *Alchemilla mollis* is invaluable to gardeners and flower arrangers as it is ultra-hardy and quick to self-seed. Its yellow-green flowers spill over edges and mingle happily with foliage plants. Here, it highlights to perfection the orange-scarlet trumpets of a near-evergreen honeysuckle.

and colour unless divided at least every three years.

Borders alter naturally as shrubs grow and take up more space and older plants die or are replaced by others. If a new plant appears weak, grows too tall or clashes with its neighbours in form or colour, move it to a better position while dormant.

▶ **Flowering foliage plants** Although hostas are primarily grown for their magnificent leaves, many are also outstanding for their erect spikes of tubular flowers. These range from white through shades of lilac and mauve and are sometimes fragrant. This handsome group thrives in light shade, the boldly ribbed hosta leaves contrasting with lacy fern fronds, the pale lilac hosta spikes with fluffy lady's mantle.

▼ **Pastel shades** Delicate colours create a restful atmosphere close to a sitting area. Feathery white astilbe plumes intermingle with pale pink crane's-bill (*Geranium endressii*) and the colour scheme is picked up and repeated by a deliciously scented, pink and white 'Ballerina' rose growing against the house wall.

▶ **Bogside companions** In early summer, the moisture-loving *Iris chrysographes* 'Black Knight' raises 60cm (2ft) tall stems of flowers which are such a deep purple colour that they appear almost black. Here, the sombre tone is lightened with drifts of double golden buttercups (*Ranunculus acris* 'Flore-pleno'). The grass-like iris foliage and the deeply cut leaves of the buttercups are in strong contrast to the ribbed hosta leaves.

◀ **Hosta associates** It is hard to beat hostas for sheer luxuriance of foliage. The Japanese species, *H. crispula*, is one of the finest, forming a dense mass of elongated, heart-shaped, ribbed leaves which are dark green with a broad margin of white. The leaves are elegantly wavy and ideally suited for massive ground-cover, seen here in late summer fronting a graceful *Fuchsia magellanica gracilis* 'Versicolor' as it droops its scarlet bells over pale mauve hosta spikes.

COLOURED COVER

**Groups of ground-cover plants
provide a dense, ornamental carpet as visually
exciting as any other association.**

Well-chosen ground-cover plants are much more than a labour-saving device for suppressing weeds. Many have beautiful flowers, and the best have attractive year-round foliage which can play an important part in any planting scheme. Moreover, the range is wide enough for all soils, seasons and situations.

Most ground-cover plants colonize ground rapidly or form tight, rounded clumps. Colonizers spread quickly, sending up suckers from a wide-spreading network of roots or rooting from stems that touch the ground. Clump-formers, such as hostas, build up more slowly but can still create a compact group of plants which cover the ground in time.

Weed-proof foliage
Many ground-cover plants have a long and vivid flowering season – rock phlox and aubrieta, for instance, are two outstanding

examples. Others, such as *Cotoneaster dammeri*, carry a handsome crop of berries in autumn and winter. But what really makes all these plants invaluable is foliage.

Evergreens are particularly important in creating ground-cover effects. Ivy, for example, has a huge range of silver and gold variegations, as well as different leaf sizes, textures and shapes.

Other 'evergreens' include plants with silvery-grey leaves which are particularly useful for introducing a lighter area of planting in shady places or to contrast with conifers or other dark-leaved plants. *Senecio* 'Sunshine' is one example, and another is *Euonymus fortunei* 'Silver Queen'. Some, such as *Gaultheria procumbens*, take on rich red tones in late summer and autumn.

Deciduous ground-cover plants are slightly less effective than evergreens in discouraging annual weeds, which can germ-

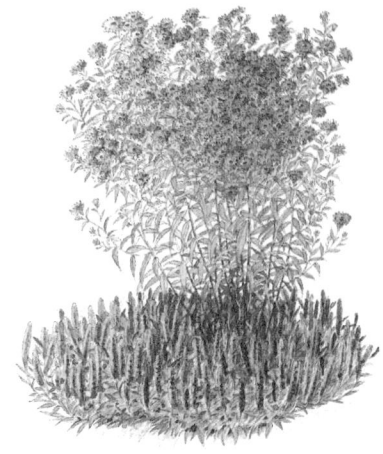

▲ **Creeping cover** The spreading stems of low-growing knotweed (*Polygonum affine*) form a dense carpet of narrow, dark green leaves that turn russet brown in autumn and persist until spring. From mid-summer to mid-autumn, the leaf carpet is topped by 20cm (8in) tall spikes of deep pink flowers, which make fine companions for blue-flowered Michaelmas daisies.

▼ **Woodland carpet** In moist shady soil, arching *Smilacina racemosa* and white-flowered *Trillium grandiflorum* provide a flowering ground-cover from late spring to early summer. Their soft colours blend well with bright azaleas.

inate before good leaf cover is produced in spring. But they do include some excellent plants, such as lungwort (*Pulmonaria* species) and *Geranium* species, which build up large clumps of splendid leaves.

Open, sunny sites

In open, sunny areas ground-cover plants can provide attractive background planting. Alternatively, they merit a place of their own for their flowers, foliage and easy-care qualities. Crane's-bills (*Geranium*), a large and beautiful group of ornamental plants, are valuable for their notched and divided leaves. The foliage dies in autumn but reappears in early or mid-spring to form close cover.

Viola cornuta, a plant with attractive, light green leaves and violet or white flowers produced abundantly over a long period, is perfect as a foil for more showy plants. The blue-flowered form provides one of the best under-plantings for beds of bush roses.

Not all open sunny positions are easy to plant – they often lack moisture. But many ground-cover plants thrive even in dry soils. *Ballota pseudodictamnus*, catmint (*Nepeta × faassenii*), *Senecio* 'Sunshine' and Spanish broom (*Genista hispanica*) are all ideal for dry and sunny sites.

Heaths and heathers are acid soil plants, although *Erica carnea* tolerates slightly alkaline soil. A mixture of heathers gives a long flowering season and the colour of the foliage – and even of the dead flowers – extends their interest.

Heavily shaded sites

Ivy is one of the most successful plants for siting beneath trees, as there is an abundance of choice in leaf colour and shape. Irish ivy (*Hedera helix* 'Hibernica') is particularly good, rapidly forming a dense cover. The silver and golden variegated forms of the common ivy (*Hedera helix*) are especially attractive; these introduce a valuable element of colour into areas of deep shade.

The yellow archangel (*Lamium galeobdolon* 'Variegatum'), with its beautifully marbled leaves, is ideal for the area beneath trees. But it grows rampantly and must be prevented from spreading as it bullies other plants in the garden out of existence.

Light or dappled shade

There are many plants to choose from, but few can match hostas for magnificent foliage. Hostas like a humus-rich soil and dislike drips from overhead leaves, but are otherwise undemanding.

Another plant worth singling out is lady's mantle (*Alchemilla mollis*). This flourishes in sun and light shade, rapidly developing mounds of large, velvety leaves and a froth of greenish-yellow flowers during spring. It is a prolific self-seeder, whose knack of fitting in between other plants makes the garden seem positively full to overflowing.

▼ **Cottage-garden charm** Old-fashioned favourites like blue-flowered lavender and silvery cotton lavender (*Santolina chamaecyparissus*) form spreading hummocks of fragrant, eye-catching cover.

▲ **Shady companions** Bugle (*Ajuga reptans*) clothes the ground with rosettes of evergreen leaves, dark purple in the form 'Atropurpurea'. It thrives in shady sites and bears blue flowers in summer. The creeping Jenny (*Lysimachia nummularia*) flourishes in similar conditions and brightens the bugle foliage with its yellow flowers.

▶ **Front-line shrubs** Small, shrubby potentillas (*Potentilla fruticosa*) provide good weed-smothering cover in large shrub borders and are almost in permanent bloom from early summer until the autumn frosts. The yellow-flowered 'Elizabeth' and the smaller, orange-coloured 'Tangerine' complement the semi-evergreen *Hypericum × inodorum* 'Elstead', resplendent in late summer with clusters of scarlet berries.

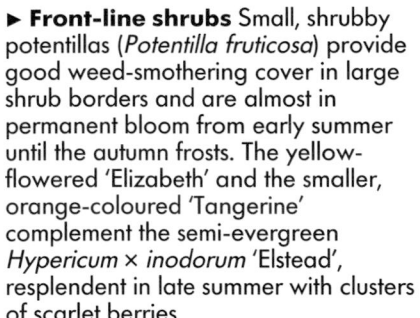

▲ **Spotted lungwort** Partial shade and moist soil suit the lungworts which spread to form distinctive ground-cover, marbled with silver in the variety *Pulmonaria saccharata*. The violet-blue flowers of the variety 'Boughton Blue' make a stunning show beneath the arching branches of white-flowered *Exochorda racemosa*.

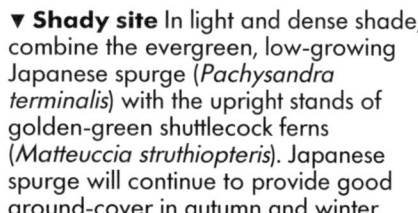

▲ **Spring colour** The dainty wake robin (*Trillium grandiflorum*) forms spreading clumps in moist shady sites, opening its three-petalled flowers in spring. White at first, they later become flushed with pink to match the developing, chestnut-like leaves of coppery *Rodgersia podophylla*.

▼ **Shady site** In light and dense shade, combine the evergreen, low-growing Japanese spurge (*Pachysandra terminalis*) with the upright stands of golden-green shuttlecock ferns (*Matteuccia struthiopteris*). Japanese spurge will continue to provide good ground-cover in autumn and winter.

► **Colourful bugles** The perennial bugle, *Ajuga reptans,* is invasive by nature and quickly covers any bare soil with its attractive leaf rosettes and small, blue flower spikes. The variety 'Burgundy Glow', in leaf colours that span metallic bronze, pink and cream, highlight the white-edged, ribbed leaves of *Hosta* 'Thomas Hogg'.

▼ **Lady's mantle** In sun or light shade, the ultra-hardy lady's mantle (*Alchemilla mollis*) spreads to form hummocks of pale green, hairy and palmate leaves. They are topped during summer by billowing sprays of delicate, lime-green flowers, invaluable for garden decoration and flower arrangements. The plants self-seed and colonize readily, and unwanted seedlings should be rooted out.

▲ **Spotted dead nettle** Near-evergreen in all but the severest of winters, the spotted dead nettle (*Lamium maculatum* 'Beacon Silver') invades nooks and odd corners to lay an ever increasing carpet of heart-shaped, green leaves flecked with silver. The hooded, purple flowers appear in late spring, and sporadically throughout the year. In order to contain the plants and to keep them neat, shear the flower heads off once the main display has finished.

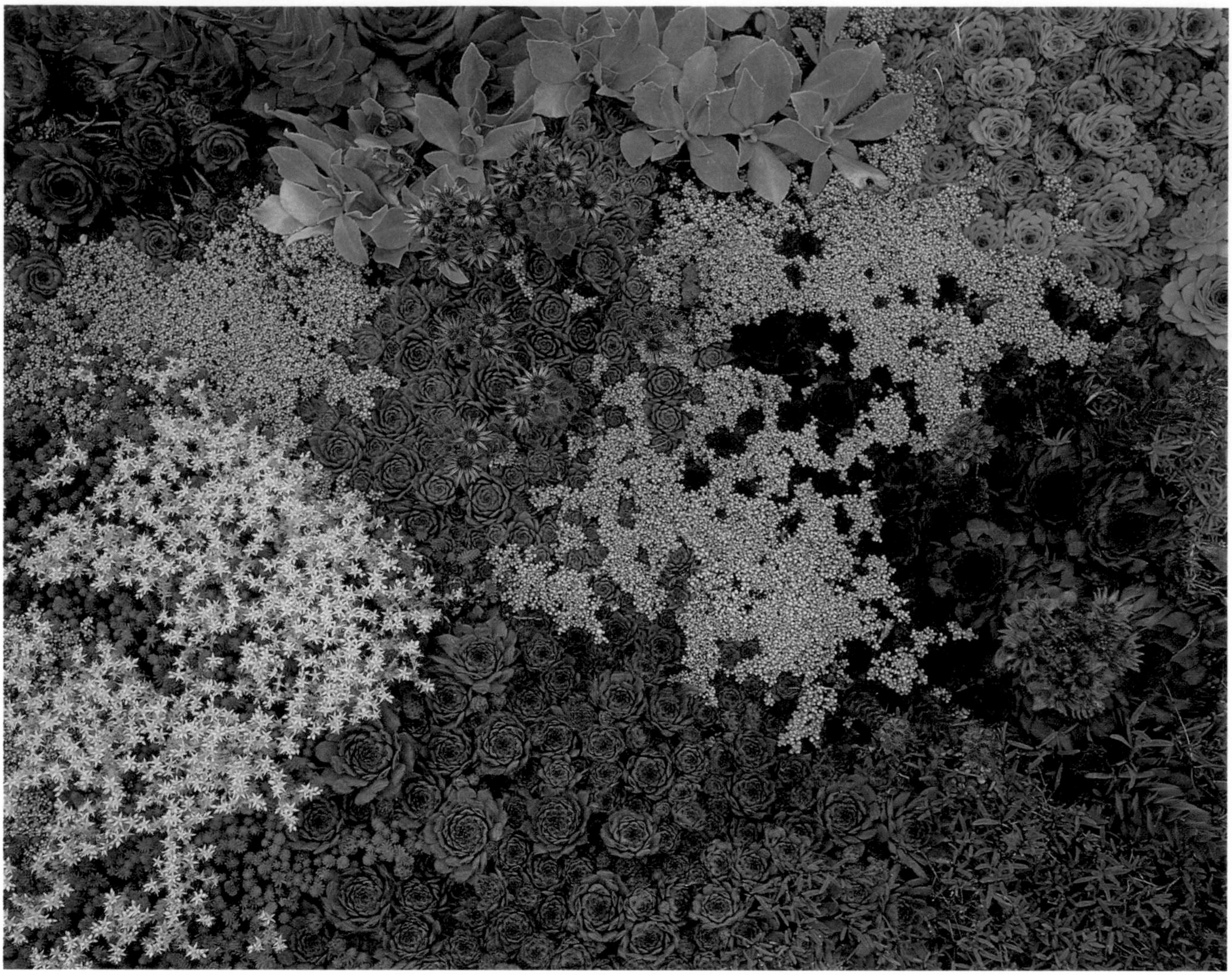

▲ **Succulent cover** Many alpines carpet soil and stones in the rock garden with ever-spreading leaf rosettes, mats and low hummocks. Here, clumps of green and purple-leaved houseleeks (*Sempervivum tectorum*) creep among mats of silvery *Raoulia hookeri* and the linear grey-green foliage of *Gypsophila repens*.

A yellow carpet of stonecrop (*Sedum acre*) ripples through the leaf cover like a pool of sunlight.

◄ **Autumn colours** The deep purple-red, fleshy leaves of a stonecrop (*Sedum maximum*) are overlaid with a bloom in the form 'Atropurpureum'. The plant spreads to form clumps which are topped in early autumn with purple-pink flower heads. In this handsome, late-summer association, the purple colour is subdued by stately, cream-white spikes of red hot poker (*Kniphofia* 'Maid of Orleans') and the yellow-green froth of ground-hugging lady's mantle (*Alchemilla mollis*).

DECORATING WITH BULBS

**With the right choice of bulbs, a
garden can come to life in autumn and winter, as well
as having a spring and summer display.**

Tulips, hyacinths and daffodils are by far the most popular bulbs, and are traditional spring features in almost every garden, but bulbs can also provide flowers in summer, autumn *and* winter. Autumn-flowering crocuses, cyclamen and nerines, for example, can brighten a garden once herbaceous perennials finish. Winter-flowering iris, snowdrops and aconites are seemingly immune to harsh weather; and lilies, including the beautiful, easy-to-grow *Lilium regale*, add beauty and scent to summer.

Even in the smallest garden, it is worth being adventurous with bulbs and corms. Many need only planting and occasional lifting and dividing. Some, such as snowdrops and crocuses, are completely carefree, and naturalize by seed and bulbils into attractive clumps or drifts.

Compared with herbaceous perennials, dormant bulbs are clean to handle and cheap to buy. Bulb catalogues offer discounts for bulk orders, especially of types

▶ **Grape hyacinth** Undemanding and easy-growing, the grape hyacinth (*Muscari armeniacum*) is ideal for naturalizing in a sunny site. Its cheerful blue flower spikes appear in mid-spring.

▼ **Autumn crocuses** Welcome for its startling splashes of colour, the autumn-flowering *Colchicum speciosum* 'Violet Queen' raises its splendid goblets well before the large and untidy leaves develop.

suitable for mass planting. Larger garden centres often have 'fill-a-bag' specials for popular bulbs – again at attractive prices.

Unlike most seeds, bulbs are easy to handle and can be placed exactly where you want them. Unless you do something drastically wrong, as many bulbs as you plant will flower, at least for the first year. Many bulbs are long-living so that they or their progeny carry on year after year – you only have to see a bluebell wood to get an idea of their tenacity.

The choice is virtually unlimited. Flower colours vary from brilliant white to subtle shades and pastels, with bi- and multi-coloured flowers in soft or quite startling combinations. Flowers can take the shape of a star, daisy, trumpet, cup or goblet; they can be single or double; held upright or gracefully nodding; and carried singly, in spikes or in many-flowered clusters.

Heights range from the ground-carpeting, diminutive *Anemone blanda*, a few centimetres high, to giant lilies (*Cardiocrinum giganteum*) 2.4m (8ft) tall, with every variation in between. Flower sizes, too, range from modest little grape hyacinths to large and showy hybrid gladioli. It's always worth studying bulb catalogues; many flamboyant hybrids have been bred from their smaller, more graceful species relatives, which are just as easy to grow.

There are flowering bulbs for sun and for shade; for hot, dry conditions and waterlogged bogs; for acid and alkaline soils, and for fertile and poor ones. In especially mild and sheltered gardens, half-hardy bulbs such as the unusual pineapple lily (*Eucomis bicolor*) and the heavily scented ginger lily (*Hedychium*) can become permanent residents.

Bulbous plants

A bulb is an organ for storing food and water, and allows a plant to remain dormant for a long time. Structurally, a bulb is a swollen leaf base holding an embryo bud; daffodils, tulips and onions are true bulbs.

Other storage organs, such as iris rhizomes, gladioli corms and cyclamen tubers, are essentially swollen stems or roots, but in terms of purpose and treatment, they are much the same as bulbs. For convenience, all are referred to as bulbs here.

In the garden, bulbs from the lily, iris and amaryllis families dominate the scene, providing all-time favourites as well as enchantingly beautiful but less well-known flowers.

Growing bulbs

Though a few bulbs, such as arums, have attractive foliage and some, such as *Iris foetidissima*, have beautiful seed pods, the vast majority are grown for their flowers.

Because modern varieties produce perfectly uniform, virtually identical plants, bulbs are popular for formal spring bedding schemes: straight-stemmed, early single tulips and Dutch hyacinths, for example, interplanted with polyanthus or forget-me-nots.

Grown informally, bulbs have a multitude of uses, from providing pockets of colour in a rock garden, to cheering up mixed beds and borders until the arrival of summer's herbaceous perennial colours. Early flowering bulbs are especially effective as underplanting, making up for the lack of colour and interest in dormant deciduous shrubs.

▼ **Bluebell glade** In late spring, the deep blue of bluebells (*Scilla nutans*) marries delightfully with the cool, fresh green of unfolding *Hosta* 'Honeybells', also blue-flowered.

◀ **Bedding tulips** Hundreds of tulip varieties are available, differing in size, shape and colour and spanning a flowering season of several months. Highly decorative types, like the double late tulip 'Peach Blossom', are most effective when massed in beds of their own kind. After flowering, they should be lifted, dried off and stored until being replanted in late autumn.

▼ **Summer bulbs** The brightly coloured Peruvian lily (*Alstroemeria* 'Ligtu Hybrids') adds an exotic touch to the summer garden. They need good soil, sun and a sheltered site in which they can be left undisturbed for years.

Bulbs planted with late-leafing perennials and shrubs, such as Japanese anemones and hardy hibiscus, give double the colour in relation to the space.

Spring bulbs can work in perfect tandem with summer bedding, filling beds with colour until half-hardy annuals and perennials such as pelargoniums, petunias and begonias come into bloom.

Daffodils, crocuses, bluebells, snowdrops and low-growing anemones and fritillaries are ideal for naturalizing, and a relatively small investment gives annually increasing returns. Crocuses and fritillaries are usually naturalized in grass, while snowdrops are ideal for growing under and around deciduous hedges as well as in grass. Bluebells and daffodils, being taller, are best naturalized in rough grass or light woodland conditions, the latter being ideal for anemones.

With the notable exception of bluebells, most bulbs will grow happily in containers: dwarf bulbs in sink gardens or half pans; larger bulbs in pots, tubs, urns and window boxes. Raised beds are essentially large-scale containers, and bulbs, especially those liking good drainage, thrive there.

Aftercare of bulbs

Some bulbs, such as tulips, degenerate if left in the ground year after year. They produce a number of bulblets, masses of foliage and fewer and fewer, smaller and smaller flowers. To prevent this

◄ **Winter joy** Few plants give as much pleasure as the little snowdrop (*Galanthus nivalis*) as it pushes its tender-green tips through hard and barren soil in the depth of winter. Its pure white, gracefully nodding bells pronounce — in spite of forbidding weather — that life in the garden is about to reawaken.

▼ **Late spring** Certain classic bedding schemes never go out of favour. Tall-stemmed tulips and multi-coloured, sweetly scented wallflowers echo the time-honoured tradition of the English garden in spring.

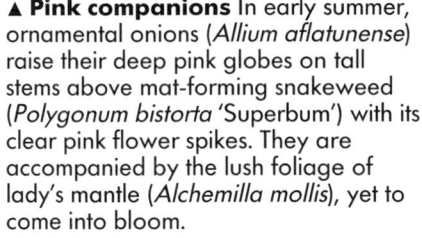

▲ **Pink companions** In early summer, ornamental onions (*Allium aflatunense*) raise their deep pink globes on tall stems above mat-forming snakeweed (*Polygonum bistorta* 'Superbum') with its clear pink flower spikes. They are accompanied by the lush foliage of lady's mantle (*Alchemilla mollis*), yet to come into bloom.

► **Winter cheer** A golden cascade of winter-flowering jasmine (*Jasminum nudiflorum*) offsets the showy, blue-flowered *Iris histrioides* sparkling among other early-flowering bulbs, which include golden *Crocus aureus*, carmine-pink *Cyclamen coum* and pure white snowdrops.

they must be lifted, stored and re-planted annually. Dutch hya-cinths can be lifted, but if left to naturalize they produce smaller, but more graceful, scented blooms.

Half-hardy bulbs, such as large-flowered gladioli, need annual lift-ing and storing to protect them from frost. An alternative is to choose smaller-flowered species,

such as *Gladiolus byzantinus* which is fully hardy.

Tall-flowering bulbs, such as gladioli, may need staking as they can often appear ungainly. How-ever, bare-stemmed, tall-flower-ing bulbs, such as alliums and lilies, may be planted where they can support themselves on shrubs or perennials.

▼ **Woodland sites** Ideal for underplanting shrubs and trees, the hardy *Cyclamen hederifolium* (syn. *C. neapolitanum*) will unfold a floral carpet from late summer until autumn, when sited in soil rich in leaf-mould and sheltered from hot sun and strong winds. The beautiful white, pale pink and mauve flowers are accompanied by deep green, heart-shaped leaves with silvery markings.

PARTNERS FOR SPRING BULBS

**Daffodils and tulips are among the best loved
of bulbs. Together with other spring bulbs, they bring colour
to the garden for several months.**

Bulbs are deservedly popular. Their flowers come in beautiful and striking colours, and in an enormous variety of shapes. In height, they range from miniatures for the rock garden, raised beds and sink gardens to 90cm (3ft) tall stately crown imperials for the rear of herbaceous borders.

Such diversity provides a wide scope for associations with other bulbous plants or with trees, shrubs and other plants.

Spring is the time for crocuses, anemones, trilliums and scillas, daffodils and narcissi, hyacinths, fritillaries and tulips to be grown in containers and window boxes, and for naturalizing in grass and bedding in formal schemes.

In very early spring, the days are brightened with snowdrops, *Cyclamen coum*, winter aconites (*Eranthis hyemalis*) and silver-blue scillas. Their pastel colours provide a

taste of warmer weather to come beneath the bare branches of wintersweet (*Chimonanthus praecox*). The lime-green flowers and evergreen foliage of *Helleborus foetidus* add height and leafy interest.

By mid-spring, sturdy-stemmed and sweet-scented hyacinths enter the picture. They can form the basis of many contrasting or harmonious bedding schemes partnered by cottage tulips, pansies and primroses, for example.

Fritillaries, too, are to the forefront by mid-spring, including the pretty snake's head (*Fritillaria meleagris*) which is equally at home in rough grass as in an undisturbed corner of the border. Its chequered purple bells could nod gracefully over a carpet of forget-me-nots and would look stunning in the company of tall, pink and purple lenten roses (*Helleborus orientalis*).

The spectacular crown imperial (*Fritillaria imperalis*), in lovely shades of yellow, orange and scarlet, could hold court over drifts of creamy American trout lilies (*Erythronium revolutum* 'White Beauty') or white-flowered narcissi. Alternatively, plant a carpet of mauve-flowered *Viola labradorica* 'Purpurea' interspersed with miniature yellow and white *Tulipa tarda* at their feet.

Partners for daffodils
Daffodils and other narcissi raise their cheerful yellow and white flowers year after year, celebrating the arrival of spring in a variety of garden situations.

▼ **Picture of spring** Large-cupped narcissi and bright, sturdy-stemmed Darwin hybrid tulips mix easily in mid spring. They are fronted by yellow *Alyssum saxatile* and white arabis.

▲ **Colour contrasts** The sweetly scented, multi-flowered Poetaz narcissus 'Geranium' blooms in late spring. Its bright orange-scarlet cups are surrounded by pure white petals. Planted in drifts beneath a deciduous tree, it is partnered by elegant, lily-flowered 'Aladdin' tulips. Their showy, pointed goblets, carmine edged with gold, offer stunning contrasts in form and colour to the softer, gently weaving narcissi.

▶ **Spring meadow** Jostling in rough grass around a moss-covered tree trunk, cheerful spring bulbs revel in each others' company. Beautifully proportioned, long-trumpeted Cyclamineus narcissi lean protectively over pure white *Anemone apennina* and miniature golden suns of the lesser celandine (*Ranunculus ficaria*). Scattered in the grass are the charming purple-chequered bells of snake's head fritillary (*Fritillaria meleagris*), which often produce white seedlings when left to colonize.

◄ **Hoop petticoats** The dainty hoop petticoat (*Narcissus bulbocodium*) is one of the first narcissi to flower. Unlike other narcissi, it often produces its yellow petticoats among winter snow. This imitation alpine meadow is backed by winter-flowering heathers (*Erica carnea*) and other narcissi, which include the 30cm (12in) tall Tenby daffodil (*Narcissus pseudonarcissus obvallaris*) with golden, frilly-edged trumpets, and the Cyclamineus narcissus 'Jack Snipe' with creamy-white petals and primrose cup.

As a complement to the heathers, rose-purple dog's tooth violets (*Erythronium dens-canis*) nod their elegant flowers among the yellow and green.

▲ **February Gold** Rarely flowering quite as early as its name would suggest, the Cyclamineus narcissus 'February Gold' with its narrow trumpets and backswept petals, is perfect for naturalizing in moist, grassy places with dappled shade.

On acid soil, its brilliant yellow trumpets associate beautifully with the deciduous *Rhododendron mucronulatum*, displaying rose-purple flowers on bare branches. Patches of bright blue, white-eyed glory-of-the-snow (*Chionodoxa luciliae*) are threaded through the narcissi clumps for subtle contrast.

▲ **Mid-spring splendour** Clumps of sturdy trumpet daffodils spread pools of sunlight over roughly-mown grass. They colonize steadily in the dappled shade of an ornamental cherry tree whose slender branches of pale pink blossom are beginning to droop downwards. Later, the fully clothed branches will help to draw the eye away from the untidy leaves of the dying daffodils.

▶ **Study in yellow** An early spring association of yellow and green is centred around the evergreen Oregon grape (*Mahonia aquifolium*). The glossy holly-like leaf clusters, which often turn red in autumn, are surmounted by dense clusters of yellow flower spikes that show up brightly in shady sites. To the rear the elegant, leafless tracery of *Corylopsis willmottiae* is hung with pale yellow catkins, while in the foreground trumpets of the wild or Lent daffodil (*Narcissus pseudonarcissus*) nod above the silver-marbled leaves of autumn-flowering *Cyclamen hederifolium*.

Sturdy trumpet daffodils, such as 'Golden Harvest' and 'Mount Hood', are ideal for containers, with pansies and hyacinths, for example.

On a larger scale, a formal bed can contain clumps of trumpet daffodils or large-cupped narcissi and a range of stiffly upright tulips. For a different flower shape, graceful Cyclamineus narcissi with backswept petals are dainty, traditional partners for the neat blue grape hyacinth.

Plant daffodils and narcissi between shrubs in mixed borders, where, after flowering, their dying foliage will be hidden by plants that come into leaf later. Or use ground-cover plants with ornamental foliage to camouflage the narcissi's browning leaves. Try silver variegated forms of *Lamium maculatum* and bronze, pink and yellow bugle (*Ajuga reptans* 'Multicolour'). White daffodils are a superb contrast for the purplish foliage of *A. reptans* 'Atropurpurea' or for the mauve blooms and purple leaves of *Viola labradorica* 'Purpurea'.

To many people, daffodils and narcissi look best planted in drifts, and naturalized in grass among the roots of deciduous trees and shrubs which come into full leaf as the bulbs finish blooming. Leave space between the groups to plant cobalt-blue, white-rimmed *Muscari armeniacum*, dog's tooth violet (*Erythronium dens-canis*), snake's head fritillary (*Fritillaria meleagris*), deep blue *Anemone apennina* and the yellowish-gold Dutch crocuses, which flourish in light shade and are excellent for naturalizing in grass.

Partners for tulips

Tulips set alone are among the most impressive of spring bulbs. But their impact is even greater when they are partnered with plants of contrasting or harmonious colours.

Perhaps the most classic partners for tulips are forget-me-nots (*Myosotis sylvatica*) and wallflowers (*Cheiranthus cheiri*). Use *Myosotis* 'Royal Blue' with tall, lemon-yellow or pink tulips.

Wallflowers look best in clumps of one colour. 'Primrose Monarch' and 'Cloth of Gold' contrast well with the maroon tulip 'Queen of the Night'. *Cheiranthus* 'Blood Red' looks stunning with white, orange or flame-coloured tulips.

In mixed borders, purple honesty (*Lunaria annua*) mixes well with 'Golden Apeldoorn' tulips, while white honesty 'Alba' is a stark contrast to maroon-black tulip goblets. For harmony, use the golden daisies of *Doronicum plantagineum* 'Miss Mason', with yellow tulips and blue grape hyacinths (*Muscari*) for extra splashes of colour.

▼ **Leaf foil** Maroon-spotted leaves are characteristic of the Greigii hybrid tulips. Blooming in mid-spring, they are partnered here by striped *Phalaris arundinacea* 'Picta'.

▲ **Rock garden tulips** The delightful little *Tulipa tarda* grows only 10cm (4in) high and is ideal for pockets of well-drained, gritty soil in a sunny rock garden. In bright sun, up to five flowers on each stem open out to form white, yellow-centred stars. It flowers in late spring at the same time as the pasque flower (*Pulsatilla vulgaris*), with its elegant, finely divided foliage and rich purple-blue flowers. A neutral background, such as greenish-grey rosemary, sets both off to perfection.

▶ **Blue and yellow** This formal bedding scheme for late spring is based on forget-me-nots, with late-flowering yellow and creamy-white tulips rising from waves of bright blue *Myosotis sylvatica* 'Blue Bird'. The blue and yellow theme is continued with an edging of low-growing, indigo-blue *Myosotis alpestris* 'Blue Ball', broken dramatically by golden *Alyssum saxatile* 'Citrinum'

▼ **Tulip partners** Kaufmanniana hybrid tulips, sometimes known as water-lily tulips, open wide in early-spring sunshine to reveal their pointed petals, usually flushed with a contrasting colour. Virginia cowslips (*Mertensia virginica*) with their drooping clusters of pure blue flowers, make admirable companions.

▶ **Early spring** The Kaufmanniana hybrid tulip 'The First' is aptly named, for this group flowers before any other tulips. Rarely more than 20cm (8in) high, it is at home in the rock garden and raised beds. Here, it opens its ivory-white, red-flushed flowers wide above the yellow blooms of evergreen, mat-forming spring cinquefoil (*Potentilla tabernaemontani*).

▶ **Gold on gold** The young, orange-red leaves of the dwarf shrub *Spiraea* × *bumalda* 'Goldflame' form a harmonious background for tall, stiff-stemmed Darwin hybrid tulips. 'Beauty of Apeldoorn' flowers in mid to late spring, with distinctive oval-shaped flowers of golden-yellow flushed with soft orange. The cool yellow flower heads of *Euphorbia polychroma* complete the sunshine picture.

▲ **Lily flowers** Pansies are traditional partners for tulips, contrasting with them in height, shape and colour. In this bedding scheme, varieties of *Viola × wittrockiana* in sumptuous regal hues pay homage to stately lily-flowered tulips. Flowering in mid and late spring, these graceful tulips have waisted flowers with long, pointed and often bicoloured petals.

◄ **Symphony in red** The typical late-flowering tulip is goblet or oval-shaped and borne on strong, stiff stems. Many Darwin hybrid tulips are bicoloured, while others come in single shades which accentuate their waxen beauty. Here, cerise-red tulips marry spectacularly with deep pink Russell lupins, their different shapes clearly highlighted.

SUMMER-FLOWERING BULBS

**The magnificent blooms of lilies and irises
are among the most beautiful of summer flowers and the
centre of attention in many partnerships.**

Many bulbous plants can be included in herbaceous and mixed borders. For instance, the Peruvian lily (*Alstroemeria* Ligtu Hybrids) in sunset colours of pink, apricot, yellow-orange and red streaked would look stunning with a backing of blue delphiniums plus yellow loosestrife (*Lysimachia punctata*) in front. Or try 1.2m (4ft) tall hyacinths (*Galtonia candicans*) against the pink and grey-green leaves of *Fuchsia magellanica* 'Versicolor' and partnered by the silver-grey foliage and magenta blooms of rose campion (*Lychnis coronaria*).

In late summer, the blue African lilies (*Agapanthus* × 'Headbourne Hybrids') associate well with the flat, yellow flower heads of *Achillea filipendulina* 'Coronation Gold'; or for striking contrast, plant the bold spikes of red hot poker (*Kniphofia*), perhaps with a foreground planting of silvery *Stachys olympica*. Also flowering in late summer are the Kaffir lilies (*Schizostylis coccinea*); their exotic, scarlet flower spikes look charming with clusters of powder-blue or creamy-white Michaelmas daisies (*Aster novi-belgii*).

Partners for irises

Their flat fans or upright grassy spears of tapering leaves and their strong-stemmed, distinctive flowers make irises one of the visual delights of the garden. Carefully chosen partners can further enhance these striking plants with their wide colour range and many forms.

Some irises are rare and difficult to grow, but in the right conditions most give little trouble. Flag irises (*Iris germanica*), for instance, are easy to grow. A background of shrubs is ideal for these – but they should not be too shaded. The pink flowers and

▶ **Summer glory** Elegant *Iris sanguinea* forms 1.2m (4ft) tall clumps of narrow, dark green foliage. Its creamy-yellow flowers calm the exuberance of pink and cerise old-fashioned roses.

▼ **Delicate colouring** A breathtaking, early-summer group has the mallow-like *Abutilon vitifolium* as its centre. The pale mauve flowers of this near-hardy shrub are complemented by pale blue *Iris pallida dalmatica* above grey-green leaf fans. Yellow tree lupins (*Lupinus arboreus*) unite the blue colours.

► **Bog garden iris** Flowering in early and mid summer, the deep purple blooms of 60cm (2ft) tall *Iris laevigata* float like exotic butterflies among lush stands of ferns. Astilbes also thrive in boggy conditions, their emerging feathery sprays delaying their flower displays until the irises have faded.

► **Tricolour scheme** Elegant 90cm (3ft) tall *Iris sibirica* raises its blue flowers against a froth of creamy-white 'Nevada' roses. Black-eyed *Geranium psilostemon* adds points of deep magenta-pink.

▲ **Hoisting the flag** Native British flowers — pale pink campion (*Silene dioica*) in the foreground and scented pink and white dame's violets (*Hesperis matronalis*) — weave a tapestry of flowers and foliage in late spring. Held regally above them are the spectacular white-bearded, purple blooms of London flag (*Iris germanica*).

◄ **Water irises** The yellow-flowered *Iris pseudacorus* will reach a height of 1.5m (5ft) in garden pools and the marshy ground by streams. Another true water iris, the shorter lavender-blue *I. laevigata*, makes a suitable companion for early-summer colour. The sword-like foliage of both plants contrasts superbly with the massive leaves of bog arum (*Lysichiton americanus*) in the background.

111

▲ **Japanese floral art** The flamboyant yet delicate iris is a popular flower in traditional Japanese floral decorations, featuring frequently as one of the three elements that are used in Ikebana arrangements.

This association emphasizes the fragile quality of the Japanese iris (*I. kaempferi*). Available in shades of blue and purple, pink, lavender and white, some forms are self-coloured, others are netted with coloured or white veins.

Mauve and white astilbe plumes reflect the colours of the Japanese iris blooms, the largest of all irises. Both plants enjoy the same conditions — moist, lime-free soil and sun.

◄ **Veiled in white** The tall, bearded iris 'Dancer's Veil' flowers in early summer, its large white blooms edged with blue-purple. Its sword-shaped foliage contrasts well with clumps of large-leaved, bluish-green *Hosta sieboldiana*, and as a background to both, the guelder rose (*Viburnum opulus*) drapes its white flowers amid green, maple-like leaves.

variegated foliage of *Weigela florida* 'Variegata' make a charming background for pale blue varieties, while the dark wine-purple foliage of the smoke bush (*Cotinus coggygria* 'Royal Purple') creates a dramatic setting for white forms.

In a mixed border, blue varieties of the taller bulbous Dutch, Spanish and English irises are beautifully enhanced by an edging of *Anthemis cupaniana*, with its white, yellow-centred daisy flowers and grey foliage.

The soft blue *Iris pallida dalmatica* makes an unusual but effective partner for another bulbous plant, the 23cm (9in) high ornamental onion (*Allium karataviense*) with its greenish white, purple-flushed flower globes and striking foliage of broad, dark green leaves suffused with purple.

A moist border is the perfect place for *I. sibirica*. The dark flowers look particularly effective with the white-margined leaves of *Hosta crispula*. At the waterside, *I. kaempferi* and *I. laevigata* are natural partners for moisture-loving rodgersia, astilbe and candelabra primulas.

Lily companions

Lilies are magnificent, stately plants with dramatic flowers and fine foliage. Lime-hating species are often planted in sunny clearings among rhododendrons and azaleas, whose foliage forms a handsome background. But provided they are not crowded out by other plants, lilies can be used successfully in mixed borders.

A group of 1m (3ft) tall *Lilium pyrenaicum*, their stems thickly set with narrow leaves and yellow Turk's-cap flowers, makes a lovely picture against a background of golden variegated *Elaeagnus pungens* 'Maculata', with the yellow-edged foliage of *Hosta fortunei* 'Aureomarginata' in front.

The pure white trumpets of lime-tolerant, sun-loving *Lilium candidum* look wonderful with the burgundy-purple old garden rose, 'Reine des Violettes'. Or, in partial shade, you could partner graceful ferns and the purple-pink *Lilium martagon* with the pinky white flowers of 60-90cm (2-3ft) high *Astrantia major*.

Orange-red Asiatic hybrids look stunning with the blues of delphiniums, *Campanula lactiflora*, the hardy geranium 'Johnson's Blue' and *Nepeta*.

Scented *Lilium regale* mixes well with yellow and buff-flowered verbascums and with *Artemisia splendens*, whose silver foliage acts as a foil to the wine-purple shading on white lily trumpets. Or, for late summer, plant apricot-orange *Lilium henryi* with purple-leaved *Atriplex hortensis* 'Rubra'.

▼ **Asiatic lily hybrids** The bright-coloured, hardy Asiatic hybrids are some of the easiest lilies to grow. The magnificent upward-facing large blooms are carried in clusters in early and mid-summer on strong leafy stems and are excellent for cutting. Colours range through shades of yellow, orange and red, sometimes spotted with black.

▲ **Regal lilies** In the warmth and shelter of a sunny wall, graceful regal lilies (*Lilium regale*) preside over blue-flowered *Agapanthus* 'Headbourne Hybrids'. Wine-red in bud, the scented lily clusters open to pure white trumpets that flare back to reveal golden throats and yellow stamens, a colour picked up by the daisy flowers of silvery-grey *Senecio* 'Sunshine' at the front of the bed.

◄ **Summer brides** For thousands of years the lily has been associated with sanctity and purity. It appears in Greek and Roman mythology and in Christian history. It was commonly featured in medieval paintings, and is the national emblem of France. Yet in spite of all the honours heaped upon it, the regal lily (*Lilium regale*) flourishes in the most ordinary of gardens. It trumpets its wax-white blooms at the height of summer, in the company of orange-pink *Alstroemeria* 'Ligtu Hybrids' and veiled in the soft white foil of baby's breath.

◄ Lilies by other names
The South African pineapple lily (*Eucomis* sp.) takes its common name from the tuft of pineapple-like bracts at the top of the sturdy flower stem. Flowering greenish-white in late summer, it contrasts in colour and form with the elegant *Lilium speciosum* whose fragrant flowers are heavily shaded with crimson on the backswept petals. Neither plant is hardy in Britain but make spectacular additions to a late-summer border, with lime-free soil, sun and shelter. Lift both types of lilies in autumn and over-winter them in a frost-free greenhouse or conservatory.

▼ Pure enchantment The golden-red 'Enchantment' lily is one of the most popular of the Asiatic hybrids. Vigorous and fully hardy, it produces its bright clusters of outward-facing blooms, each up to 15cm (6in) across, in high summer year after year. It flourishes in full sun, with some shade over the root area, here provided by a mini-forest of evergreen, pale blue lavender (*Lavandula angustifolia*).

◄ **Madonna lily** Named after the Virgin Mary and depicted in innumerable religious paintings, the Madonna lily (*Lilium candidum*) has been in cultivation for thousands of years. Once established in ordinary soil with full sun, it will unfold its miraculous blooms in early summer. The fragrant, funnel-shaped flowers are of the purest white with golden centres, and associate particularly well with grey or purple-leaved herbs and shrubs. Here, the smoke tree (*Cotinus coggygria* 'Royal Purple') makes a dramatic backcloth for the lilies. Later, their place will be taken by the mauve-tinted, white flowers of *Clematis viticella* 'Alba' scrambling through the shrub.

▼ **Favourite friends** Roses and lilies form classic partnerships as their main flowering season in mid-summer coincides. Good associations use colours that blend harmoniously without detracting from each other. Here, palest yellow roses take on lustre from orange-red Asiatic hybrid lilies, whose flamboyance is toned down by the coolness of the roses.

PORTABLE PARTNERS

Plants in pots and containers increase the opportunities for colourful partnerships and make it easier to cultivate difficult plants.

There are many advantages in growing plants in pots, whatever the size and layout of a garden. In some cases, the special needs of a plant can be met only by confining it to a pot. In other cases, container growing makes caring for plants easier. Plants in pots can also be used to conceal eyesores, or they can be moved around like stage props, to create a series of ever-changing garden pictures.

Garden limitations
If you have a balcony, courtyard or roof garden, growing plants in pots is almost the only option. (Overhanging climbing plants is the only other practical alternative.) Concrete areas outside urban basement flats are also container gardens from necessity. But those that are well planned can be so leafy and flowery that, looking down on them from street level, none of the pots are visible.

Window boxes, wall-hung pots and hanging baskets are often the only claim to a garden for flat dwellers. Fortunately, plant breeders and garden centres have responded to the growing demand by offering an ever-increasing range of scaled-down colourful plants which are perfect for containerized growing.

Provided you use sterilized potting compost – not garden soil – weeds and soil pests are all but eliminated in container gardening – though the odd woodlouse may creep in through drainage holes.

▼ **Colour step by step** A procession of container-grown annuals and bedding plants turns a flight of steps into a landscape of colour. Annuals planted in the cavity walls create unity.

▲ **Spring garden** A stylish window box always attracts attention. Permanent features like miniature conifers can be enlivened with spring bulbs and dwarf cinerarias and in summer with colourful annuals.

◄ **Colour co-ordinates** Cool white and yellow annuals echo the colours of the trellis and seating and form an enchanting transition to the garden.

► **Specimen plants** A spiky-leaved Cordyline palm underplanted with pelargoniums and silvery helichrysums creates an instant focal point.

Containerized plants are more easily relocated than their flower-bed counterparts – a thought to bear in mind when moving house. People become attached to their plants, but it can be difficult to uproot prized specimens. Containerized plants can be moved with the furniture, to give a new home an instantly welcoming feel.

Cultural needs
Certain popular summer plants – tender fuchsias, pelargoniums and wax begonias – need winter protection. They can be bedded out in late spring, and potted up in autumn to overwinter indoors, but it is easier to keep them in pots, and move them in or out, as and when the need arises.

wall into a vertical garden. On a more temporary note, you might want to 'dress' up the garden for an outdoor party, using pots of colourful plants.

Although some pots have no inherent beauty, many terracotta, wood, glass-fibre 'lead', stone or concrete containers are attractive in their own right, and contrast well with plants.

Wide, flat-topped walls, whether retaining or freestanding, can be enhanced by a collection of pot-grown plants. If you set dwarf or alpine plants in wall-mounted pots, you can enjoy their beauty at close quarters without having to stoop to ground level. Provided a path is wide enough, a row of pots can be used as edging or, if width allows, to line garden steps on one or both sides. One huge pot placed at the end of a path, or at the junction of a flower bed and lawn, makes an attractive marker for boundary and level changes. A pair of matching pots placed either side of a gate or doorway reinforces symmetry and lends an air of formal dignity to the most ordinary entrance.

Plant-filled pots can conceal as well as enhance: a manhole cover, broken paving slab, bathroom window or an ugly bit of walling can completely disappear beneath or behind potted plants.

Choosing short-term plants

Annuals are ideal plants for pots, and are available ready grown, so you can have instant colour from late spring until mid-autumn. Spring-flowering biennials, such as wallflowers, forget-me-nots, Canterbury bells and double daisies, are also suitable for containers. Some, such as wallflowers, have small root systems compared to their top growth, so they put on a good display even in small pots.

Bulbs, such as tulips, daffodils, hyacinths and grape hyacinths, are delightful for 'potted' spring colour. With biennials and spring bulbs, it is sensible to buy and plant in autumn. They can also be bought in flower in spring for planting out, though they are much more expensive then, and you forfeit the pleasure of watching them grow and develop. The same is true for winter-flowering irises, which should be planted in early autumn. Pots of summer-flowering lilies can provide fragrance as well as magnificent

Some alpine plants tolerate low winter temperatures but not the wet soil and damp atmosphere that go with them. These, too, are best grown in pots or in special shallow alpine pans and overwintered in an unheated greenhouse.

You may yearn to grow azaleas, rhododendrons, camellias and summer-flowering heathers but garden on alkaline, chalky soil which precludes cultivation of these acid-loving plants. It *is* possible to build raised peat beds or fill in planting holes with a peat substitute mixture and treat the plants frequently with sequestrene, but eventually the underlying soil will reassert its alkaline nature. It is much more sensible to grow the plants in suitable containers filled with a proprietary ericaceous compost.

Some plants grow better in pots than in open ground. Figs, for example, produce more fruit when grown where their roots are restricted than when they are allowed to roam freely. Certain rampant plants, such as mint, are also better grown in pots to prevent them overrunning the garden.

Decorating with pot plants

Even in gardens with plenty of open ground and ideal soil, there is scope for plants in pots. A large expanse of patio, for example, can benefit from the softening effect of plants in pots. A pot-grown climber trained up trellising can transform a bare house or garden

blooms – again planted while dormant or bought in flower for instant display.

Herbaceous perennials, such as hostas, acanthus and agapanthus, grow happily and look beautiful in pots, but they die back in autumn and remain dormant until spring. Unless you have an out-of-the-way spot to store them, it is better to choose evergreen perennials, such as periwinkles, bergenias or Christmas roses, or forego perennials altogether.

Lastly, there are many house plants, such as palms, passion flowers, jasmines, spider plants, cacti and succulents, that enjoy a summer stint outdoors, between the last spring frost and the first autumn one. Summer showers clean the dust off their leaves, and whitefly are less troublesome outdoors. Some flowering house plants, such as oleanders and orange and lemon trees, benefit from exposure to summer sun; it ripens their wood and helps to encourage the production of next year's flowers.

Long-term plants
While herbaceous plants and house plants add short-term colour, woody plants add substance to a garden. Shrubs and trees in pots are doubly important if there are none in the open ground. Always try to match the size of the container to the needs of the long-term plant. You can, with bonsai-like regimes of topping and

▲ **Circular theme** A giant container planted with *Erysimum* 'Bowles Mauve', a perennial with wallflower-like flowers in late spring, creates an impressive focal point, sitting like the hub of a wheel in a circle of sunken-brick paving. The circular bed at the base is filled with pansies and London Pride (*Saxifraga* x *urbium*), and the lines of a low, neatly trimmed box hedge emphasize the formal scale of the centrepiece.

▶ **Potted bay** Standard-trained bay laurels (*Laurus nobilis*), here clipped into pyramid shapes, are traditional pot-grown subjects. They provide height without taking up too much ground space. The large, pre-treated wooden tubs, filled with good potting compost, are mounted on castors to facilitate moving them around.

▶ **Formal approach** Urns brimming with geraniums and fuchsias add colour to sentinels of round-clipped box and standard, potted bay trees.

root-pruning, feeding and watering, keep potentially huge trees and shrubs small, but it is more sensible to choose plants that can reach their optimum size in the container provided.

So many trees and shrubs are happy to grow in pots that there is no reason to struggle with difficult plants. Camellias, box, aucuba, bay, fatsia, heathers, cordyline, hollies, euonymus, lavender, rhododendrons, rosemary, skimmia, senecio and laurustinus are suitable broad-leaved evergreens. For deciduous shrubs, choose from Japanese maples, ribes, cotoneasters, ceanothus, St. John's wort, hydrangeas and mock oranges.

Large, semi-mature trees can be grown in the type of planters that are often used outside public buildings, but many smaller standard trees will thrive in domestic-sized tubs, such as half beer barrels. These include box elder, winter-flowering cherry, ornamental crab apples, sorbus, the dwarf weeping Kilmarnock willow, gleditsia and several fruit trees.

Standard rose trees in pots are a traditional summer feature, but they look so grim during the winter that shrub roses of the so-called patio type might be a better choice for a small garden.

Low-growing conifers, such as horizontal junipers, can be most attractive in tubs, and there are many dwarf forms of larger conifers, including dwarf cedars and spruces. It is best to avoid fast-growing conifers, which can get leggy at the base.

For pots against walls, don't forget woody climbers: clematis, wisteria, honeysuckle, jasmine, Virginia creeper, Russian vine, ivy and climbing roses. In terms of scale, pot-grown climbers often put on the biggest display of all.

Care and maintenance
Plants growing in pots are usually

▶ **Cheerful informality** A cottage door is almost obscured by hanging baskets, boxes, wall pots and tubs. Busy Lizzies, pelargoniums, trailing fuchsias and lobelias, marigolds and wax begonias create a riot of colour.

◄ **Miniature garden** An old boot cast in a concrete mould sprouts a miniature garden. Colourful rosettes of evergreen, succulent houseleeks (*Sempervivum*) thrive in the minimum of well-drained soil and in full sun.

frequent watering in summer. Sheltered spots are always better than exposed sites, as wind has a drying or physically damaging effect on foliage and flowers.

Appearance Dead-heading and the removal of faded flowers or damaged leaves and awkwardly placed or broken branches keep a display looking good. Replacing spring flowers, such as double daisies and forget-me-nots, with summer ones is an annual task, but from time to time you may also need to use 'infill' plants to close gaps created by plants that failed to take. Lobelia, alyssum or sprigs of ivy are easy, cheap fillers.

Use a nail brush and warm soapy water to scrub off any algae that forms on pots in shade. Plants placed in partial shade – against a wall, for example – will grow towards the light and end up lop-sided unless the pots are turned regularly to distribute sunlight equally.

Plant mixtures
Whether you mix plants or grow them singly in containers is entirely a matter of taste. Single, formally trained specimen bays or clipped topiary box often look more impressive on their own, as living sculptures. The same applies to large-scale rosette-type plants, such as agave, cordyline or palm. Given their grand overtones, a circle of dwarf annuals round the base can look out of place; a gravel or woodbark mulch to conceal the compost is all that is needed. Standard fuchsias, however, can look beautiful with an underplanting of annuals.

Mixed planting for summer colour can create a pleasantly informal effect. Certain mixtures are traditional favourites: for example, fuchsias, trailing lobelia and petunias; and pelargoniums, silver-leaved senecio and alyssum. When mixing bedding plants, make sure they have the same soil, feeding, watering and light requirements. In shady spots, for example, ferns, ivies, begonias, calceolarias, Herb Robert and busy Lizzies all like the same conditions.

more dependent on human care than those growing in the open ground, so it is important to give them the best possible start and to meet their ongoing needs.

Drainage Except for water-loving plants, such as water-lilies, sweet flag or cyperus, adequate drainage is essential. All pots should have at least one good-sized drainage hole. For loam-based composts, line the container with a 2.5cm (1in) thick layer of pebbles or broken clay flower pot pieces. (This is less important for peat-based compost.)

Feeding Follow the same routine as for plants grown in open ground, but never apply liquid fertilizer to dry soil. Plants grown for foliage appreciate fertilizers high in nitrates, while those grown for flowers benefit most from potash-high fertilizers. With mixed planting, use a balanced, all-purpose fertilizer, such as Growmore. In pots, overfeeding is far more liable to be a problem than underfeed-ing, so stick to the manufacturers' recommended doses. It is safer still to use slow-releasing organic fertilizers.

Watering Plants dry out quicker in pots than in the open ground, and annuals, especially, need frequent watering in hot weather, sometimes twice a day. With peat-based composts, you may have to soak the whole pot in water in really dry weather. Otherwise, water runs down the inside of the pot and out through the drainage holes before the compost can absorb it. Many plants enjoy being mist-sprayed as well, in the evening or early morning.

Aspect Plants grown in pots need exactly the same light or shade as they would if grown in open ground. In addition, plants in pots are less protected from extremes of temperature, whether baking sun or freezing cold, than their open-grown counterparts. This may mean lagging permanent pots in winter to keep frost off the roots, or

Rock, wall and water plants

Despite their name, rock plants don't need rocks at all, merely well-drained soil of a specific acidity or alkalinity and bright sun or dappled shade, just like any other plant. This means there is no need to build an elaborate rock garden to grow alpine plants successfully. They will thrive on the flat, but because they are naturally low in stature, the beauty of their flowers is often lost at ground level. Raised beds, sinks and troughs bring them nearer to eye level, and many of the more common types – aubrieta and alyssum, for example – spill colourfully over ledges and walls while houseleeks colonize nooks and crannies with the minimum of soil. At the other end of the scale are the sometimes 'difficult' high-alpine plants like the blue-trumpeted gentians. Some grow happily in ordinary garden conditions while others such as *Gentiana acaulis* can test the gardener's skills.

A wide range of beautiful rock garden plants lie between these two extremes – perennials, miniature bulbs and dwarf shrubs. There are mat-forming evergreens like the saxifrages that flower in winter, dwarf shrubs such as the sweet-scented daphnes, and slow-growing miniature conifers – spreading junipers, globular cryptomerias and dome-shaped spruces.

Water – still pools, running streams and cascading fountains – adds a special appeal to a garden. It contributes movement, light and sound, and suitable conditions for true aquatics that grow with their feet in water and bog plants that flourish in moisture-retentive soil. Still water provides a suitable environment for plants of opposing habits: the tall vertical lines of water irises, reeds and rushes, and the floating pads and beautiful cups of water lilies. Careful juxtaposing of these two opposites gives scope for many successful partnerships.

Alpine carpets An imitation rocky landscape is covered with alpines, purple Jacob's ladder and white columbines.

ROCKERY PARTNERS

**Alpines combine well with small bulbs, dwarf
shrubs and plants renowned for their carpet-forming habit
to form scenes of natural charm in rockeries.**

The many delightfully flowered dwarf plants that grow naturally on mountains and on rugged terrain are collectively called alpines or rock garden plants. Compact growth, arguably their most striking feature, is an adaption to harsh and unsympathetic conditions, particularly fierce, drying winds.

These small plants display a variety of interesting shapes. There are the neat, rounded cushions, buns and hummocks of thrift, dianthus and certain saxifrages which contrast extremely well with the jagged forms of a rockery. There are the encrusted saxifrages, lewisias, and sempervivums with their distinctive rosette forms. In addition, there are vigorous carpet-forming species (aubrietas, cerastium and thymes) that tumble over rocks.

Perennials, deciduous, evergreen and coniferous shrubs and sub-shrubs (plants which are woody without developing the full woody growth of true shrubs) which fit into the alpine category include many popular plants that are both rewarding and undemanding to grow. Aubrieta, rock rose and thrift, for example, flourish and flower profusely provided they are given well-drained soil and full sun.

Other rock garden plants have special requirements. They need free drainage but also require a plentiful supply of water and protection from excess moisture during winter. High-altitude alpines such as gentians, rock jasmine and certain primulas are particularly demanding.

Between the two extremes are a wide range of rock garden plants that vary in habit, flowering season, flower type and colour.

Most garden centres and nurseries have a section completely devoted to rock garden and alpine plants. Although the choice is limited to easy-growing types, they are among the most free flowering and are therefore ideal for a first selection. For a wider choice of plants, consult a specialist nursery.

Rock garden plants are usually sold in small pots and can be

▼ **Spring in the rock garden** The high season for the majority of alpine plants is mid and late spring. Mats of red and purple *Aubrieta deltoidea* and gold dust (*Alyssum saxatile*) tumble over rock ledges, with clumps of mossy saxifrages and startling white *Arabis caucasica* 'Flore Pleno' adding paler colours to the spring scene.

► **Mid-summer partners** Capturing the essence of a Mediterranean hillside, these alpines thrive in a sunny rock garden. The evergreen stone orpine (*Sedum reflexum*) forms a miniature forest, 20cm (8in) high, of bright yellow, long-stalked flower heads above a ground-cover of wild thyme (*Thymus praecox arcticus*, syn *T. drucei*).

The common form of thyme has rose-purple flowers and aromatic leaves, but varieties with white, pink, lilac or crimson flowers are also available.

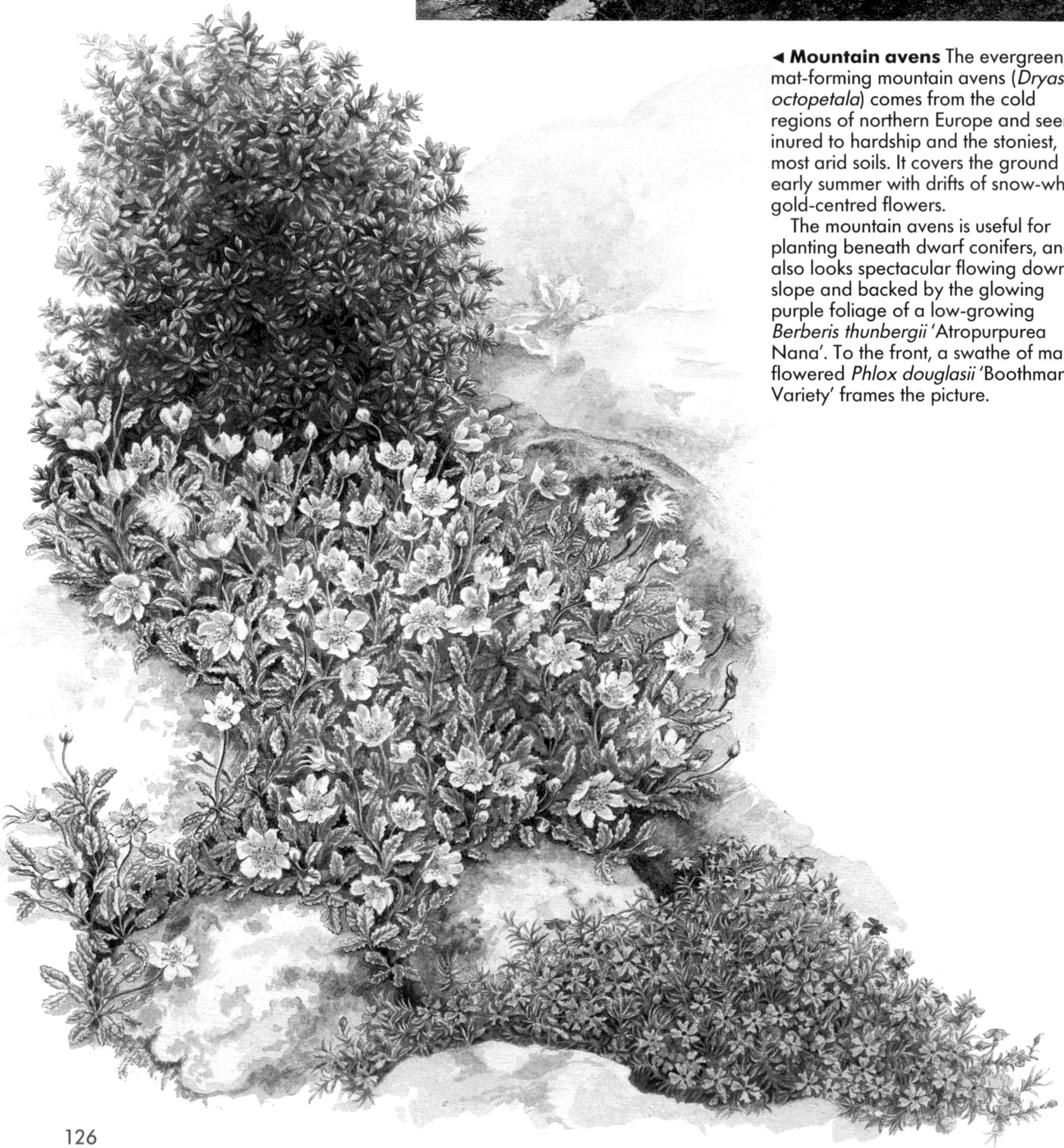

◄ **Mountain avens** The evergreen, mat-forming mountain avens (*Dryas octopetala*) comes from the cold regions of northern Europe and seems inured to hardship and the stoniest, most arid soils. It covers the ground in early summer with drifts of snow-white, gold-centred flowers.

The mountain avens is useful for planting beneath dwarf conifers, and also looks spectacular flowing down a slope and backed by the glowing purple foliage of a low-growing *Berberis thunbergii* 'Atropurpurea Nana'. To the front, a swathe of mauve-flowered *Phlox douglasii* 'Boothman's Variety' frames the picture.

planted at any time, weather permitting. During hot and dry spells, give the young plants plenty of water.

Seasonal colour

Since the most robust rock garden plants are often the most free-flowering, the return is stunning for little effort. In creating rock garden partnerships, remember that vigorous carpet-forming species look effective planted above a ledge where they can cascade over the rock face. Avoid placing them too near slower-growing mounded or tufted plants as they will soon crowd them out. The less vigorous species, however, look best intermingled to form irregular drifts. Plant the gaps between rocks with rosette-type species which will slowly spread to fill the spaces.

Creating year-round interest in a rockery is not difficult. Dwarf conifers, available in prostrate, bun, conical and upright shapes, are a useful mainstay, while evergreen foliage can be provided by the succulent green or purple rosettes of houseleeks (*Sempervivum*) and by the ground-hugging *Arabis ferdinandii-coburgii* 'Variegata'.

▶ **Dwarf conifers** Slow-growing conifer spires in gold and dark green take summer colour from alpine pinks, aubrietas, golden alyssum and bedding clumps of dwarf busy Lizzies.

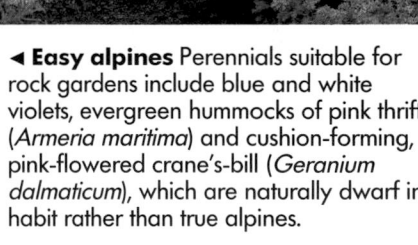

◀ **Easy alpines** Perennials suitable for rock gardens include blue and white violets, evergreen hummocks of pink thrift (*Armeria maritima*) and cushion-forming, pink-flowered crane's-bill (*Geranium dalmaticum*), which are naturally dwarf in habit rather than true alpines.

In early spring, bronze-leaved, pink-flowered *Primula* × 'Garryarde Guinevere' and blue *Hepatica nobilis* will create a beautiful association in semi-shaded spots.

You can achieve bold patches of colour simply by growing the strongest of the rock garden plants that, like aubrieta, are of spreading habit. The best for spring colour are *Aethionema* × 'Warley Rose', yellow alyssum (*Alyssum saxatile*), dwarf species and cultivated forms of phlox (such as *Phlox douglasii*) and thrift (*Armeria maritima*).

Before these have finished flowering, the mossy saxifrages begin – a haze of dainty white,

pink or deep red flowers covering hummocks of neat green leaves.

A recent introduction, *Diascia* × 'Ruby Field', with unusual pink flowers, provides a long summer display. Extend the flowering season by cutting the plants back after the first flowering.

Rock roses (*Helianthemum nummularium*) also offer many attractive summer colours ranging from soft pinks and yellows to deep oranges and reds.

Other summer-flowering plants to consider are *Silene schafta*, whose pink flowers continue well into autumn, a lovely blue spreading speedwell (*Veronica prostrata*) and any of the aromatic thymes (such as *Thymus drucei*). The 15cm (6in) high alpine asters (*Aster alpinus*) are lovely for summer colour with their yellow-eyed lavender or purple-blue daisy flowers, which are pure white in the variety 'Albus' and clear blue in 'Beechwood'.

For late summer, a blue and yellow grouping could feature the St John's wort (*Hypericum olympicum*) and the clumpy *Campanula carpatica* with its large blue cups. *Gentiana septemfida* could be planted nearby to introduce a touch of intense blue. Then, in front you could have yellow-flowered *Sisyrinchium brachypus*.

▲ **Pasque flower** Supposedly flowering at Easter, the pasque flower (*Pulsatilla vulgaris*) is a plant from chalky lowlands which settles happily in well-drained soil in sunny rock gardens and raised beds. The variety 'Baron's Pink' is spectacular in bloom.

▼ **Study in purple** Gold-centred purple-blue pasque flower (*Pulsatilla vulgaris*) also comes in red, pink and white varieties. In this mid-spring association, it is joined by the lime-green bracts of euphorbias and clumps of arching blue grass (*Festuca glauca*).

▲ **Harbingers of spring** In pale winter sunlight, the purity of simple, well-loved flowers heralds the awakening of new life. Pale lilac goblets of *Crocus tommasinianus* shimmer in a rock-garden pocket, illuminating the incomparable pale yellow of the first primroses (*Primula vulgaris*) and the last drooping bells of snowdrops (*Galanthus nivalis*).

▲ **Pools of purple** In this charming miniature rock landscape, twin peaks of compact, slow-growing junipers (*Juniperus communis* 'Compressa') rise from a sea of naturalized purplish-blue *Anemone blanda*.

▶ **Alpine carpet** You can create an alpine lawn by planting a rock garden with varieties of wild thyme (*Thymus drucei*). They will knit together to form a flowering carpet throughout summer, with evergreen foliage cover for the rest of the year. Intermingled here are pale pink 'Annie Hall' in the foreground, white 'Albus' in the centre, and lilac 'Lanuginosa' at the back. Here and there, the carpet is broken by clumps of purple *Aster alpinus*, lavender *Viola cornuta* and pink *Geranium dalmaticum*. Silky seed heads of *Pulsatilla vulgaris* rise above the alpine 'turf'.

▶ **Garland flowers** Every rock garden should include a garland flower (*Daphne cneorum*). This dwarf evergreen shrub is often temperamental, but once established it is so glorious that it is worth persevering. It resents root disturbance, so start with a young, pot-grown specimen which will eventually spread to several square feet. It is smothered in early summer with richly scented, pink flowers, deeper and richer in the form 'Eximia'.

Such pink swathes are merely enhanced by the silvery leaves of the dwarf evergreen shrub *Euryops acraeus* — with yellow daisy flowers in high summer — and contrast magnificently with the graceful spikes of airy St Bernard's lily (*Anthericum liliago*).

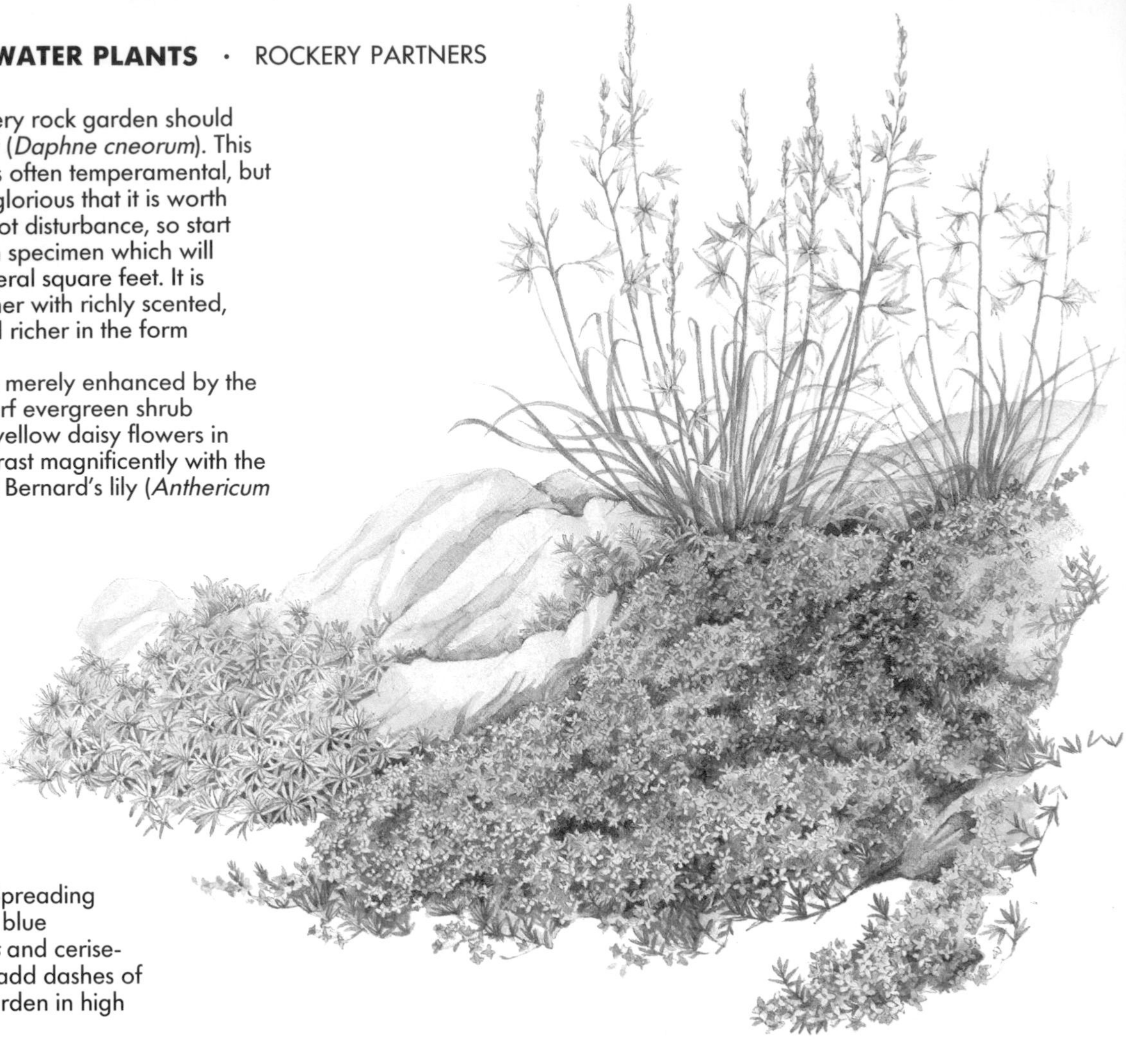

▼ **Summer opulence** Spreading clumps of bell-flowered, blue *Edraianthus serpyllifolius* and cerise-pink *Penstemon alpinus* add dashes of vivid colour to a rock garden in high summer.

Astilbe chinensis var. *pumila*, 30cm (12in) in height, has feathery pink blooms in early autumn, which are perfectly echoed by the evergreen knotweed (*Polygonum vacciniifolium*), a plant with rose-pink pokers. Complete the scheme with the silver leaves of *Artemisia schmidtiana* 'Nana'.

Choice alpines

Many distinctive rock garden plants grow in tufts or form neat clumps. Their attractive foliage is often a feature in its own right.

One of the loveliest examples is the pasque flower (*Pulsatilla vulgaris*), so called because its flowering season coincides with Easter. The clump of finely divided foliage appears early in spring when downy buds open to show golden-centred mauve or purple flowers.

Some groups of plants are particularly rich in distinctive species or varieties and are well worth planting in a collection of any size. Four that make a good starting point are alpine pinks (*Dianthus*), true geraniums, primulas and gentians.

The alpine pink (*Dianthus alpinus*) forms a neat, dense hummock which is quite obscured in summer by a generous display of single

flowers whose petals have serrated edges. This species, available in a number of varieties, looks equally lovely in a rock garden, raised bed or as part of a trough collection.

Geranium dalmaticum is one of the easiest dwarf geraniums to grow. It forms a mat of foliage smothered by pink flowers in midsummer. It thrives in poor conditions, making a good living even in cracks between paving.

Primulas combine simplicity with elegance. They do best in light shade and like moist conditions and a plentiful supply of humus. *Primula frondosa*, for

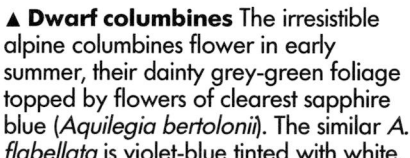

▲ **Dwarf columbines** The irresistible alpine columbines flower in early summer, their dainty grey-green foliage topped by flowers of clearest sapphire blue (*Aquilegia bertolonii*). The similar *A. flabellata* is violet-blue tinted with white.

example, responds well to a generous addition of leaf-mould to the soil, giving a spring display of golden-eyed, rose-pink flowers.

Gentians typify the beauty of alpines. Many have a reputation for being temperamental but one, *Gentiana septemfida*, produces a mass of rich blue flowers in summer without special attention. It does best in rich, moist soil.

Cracks and crevices

Plants from the other extreme – those requiring sharp drainage – often do best when grown in crevices, and they give life and beauty to vertical stone faces.

Stonecrops and houseleeks (*Sedum* and *Sempervivum* species) are some of the easiest plants to grow. The succulent leaves of houseleeks in particular are wonderfully marked, giving a year-round display of greater value than the flowers.

The Kabschia group of saxifrages include many delightful miniatures. One of the very best of these is *Saxifraga* × 'Jenkinsae', with pale pink flowers in early spring.

In alkaline soil the leaves of *S.* × 'Jenkinsae' are often encrusted

◄ **Succulent alpines** A Mexican desert effect has been achieved by placing pots of purple-leaved echeverias and tapering agaves among hardy rock garden plants. These include carpets of variegated arabis and thymes, feathery *Artemisia schmidtiana* 'Nana' and clumps of sempervivums and *Sedum* 'Rosea'.

131

◀ **Alpine tapestry** Many true rock garden plants can be mixed with dwarf perennials and spring-flowering bulbs. The plants in this flowering meadow are identified in the key above.

1 Violets (*Viola* hybrids)
2 Alpine wallflower (*Erysimum alpinum*)
3 Mossy saxifrage (*Saxifraga* hybrid)
4 Aubrieta (*Aubrieta deltoidea*)
5 Gold-dust (*Alyssum saxatile*)
6 Perennial candytuft (*Iberis sempervirens*)
7 Primrose (*Primula vulgaris*)
8 Grape hyacinth (*Muscari armeniacum*)
9 Fleabane (*Erigeron × hybridus*)
10 Leopard's bane (*Doronicum plantagineum*)
11 Daffodil (*Narcissus* variety)

with granules of lime, making them sparkle and glisten.

Foliage effects

It is a good idea to include some larger plants – shrubs and dwarf conifers – in the rock garden. They add height and substance, linking the smaller plants and preventing a disjointed effect. Many, such as broom (*Cytisus × kewensis*), have beautiful flowers.

The garland flower (*Daphne cneorum*) – best known for its wonderful show of scented pink flowers – has evergreen foliage which is welcome in the winter.

The most useful varieties of conifer are the dwarf forms of false cypress (*Chamaecyparis*) and Noah's Ark tree (*Juniperus communis* 'Compressa'), which has tight upright growth.

▶ **Trumpeting gentians**
Breathtakingly blue, the high-alpine gentians are invaluable for late-spring colour. The large trumpets of *Gentiana acaulis* flare next to the star-like spring gentians (*G. verna*). Both rise above grey-leaved *Saxifraga* 'Valerie Finnis'.

WALL COMMUNITIES

House walls offer scope for sympathetic colour associations, while free-standing and retaining walls are home to alpines that almost do without soil.

The shelter and reflected warmth of walls protect those more delicate shrubs and plants that are often unreliably hardy in the open. Bare walls can be unattractive, even depressing, but when covered with climbers and fronted with shrubs, flowers and bulbs, they blend into the garden, becoming a beautiful vertical element.

Sunny south and west-facing walls are ideal for such half-hardy shrubs as *Abutilon × suntense* 'Violetta', whose rich purple flowers make a striking partnership with the lemon-yellow *Fremontodendron* 'California Glory'. The many rock roses (*Cistus*) and Californian lilacs (*Ceanothus*) enjoy similarly protected positions. The fluffy blue flowers of *Ceanothus thyrsiflorus* 'Cascade' look charming in late spring and early summer with the white-flowered *Clematis montana* 'Wilsonii' scrambling through them.

Various colour schemes can be created with large-flowered clematis, such as white 'Marie Boisselot' and lavender-coloured 'W. E. Gladstone'. But they are most eye-catching when mingled with shrubs whose flowers are of contrasting shape.

Climbing roses are perfect partners for clematis. For contrast, plant *C.* 'Jackmanii Superba' with 'Golden Showers' or, for harmony, with the sweetly scented, pink-flowered 'New Dawn'.

Grey and silver-leaved plants, such as lavender, cotton lavender and *Euphorbia characias wulfenii*, like warmth and can provide a foil both for larger background shrubs and front plantings of, for instance, colourful South African daisies such as *Gazania, Gerbera, Venedio-arctotis* and the star-shaped *Dimorphotheca*.

▶ **Stone walls** The beautiful mellow appearance of real stone walls demands restrained embellishments. Cool green colours are in fine keeping with grey stonework, a theme complemented by the white flower heads of climbing *Hydrangea petiolaris*. Like the hostas in front, hydrangea thrives in shady, north-facing sites.

Shady walls

Garrya elliptica is one of the climbers and wall shrubs which accept shade and bring an otherwise gloomy aspect to life. Its festoons of lime-green catkins in mid winter could be brightened by the yellow stars of *Jasminum nudiflorum*. In early summer the creamy white lace-cap blooms of the climbing *Hydrangea petiolaris* can be partnered by the butter-yellow flowers of the honeysuckle, *Lonicera tragophylla*.

The evergreen, climbing *Akebia-quinata*, with its clusters of fragrant, chocolate-purple flowers in mid-spring, thrives on north-facing walls and associates handsomely with dwarf *Drimus winteri* var. *andina*, whose white flowers open slightly later.

That splendid fruiting shrub, the staff vine (*Celastrus orbiculatus*) is another good subject for a shady wall. It doesn't need a partner, except perhaps for a green-leaved ivy as background for its rounded leaves which turn yellow in autumn. This is when

◄ **Sunny shelter** The Californian tree poppy (*Romneya coulteri*) is a shrubby perennial that is cut back to the ground in autumn. It is temperamental and resents disturbance, but in the warmth and shelter of a south-facing wall produces scented, white flowers with petals crinkled like taffeta.
It flowers during late summer, and ideal half-hardy companions include blue *Agapanthus* 'Headbourne Hybrids' and the white-trumpeted *Crinum × powellii* 'Album'. Trained against the wall and framing the picture is a purple and white passion flower.

▲ **Wall dressing** An unattractive brick wall has become a beautiful focal point where the foliage of *Cotinus coggygria* 'Royal Purple' backs the pale pink, carmine-barred flowers of *Clematis* 'Nellie Moser'. Honeysuckle (*Lonicera periclymenum* 'Belgica') weaves its cream trumpets between them.

▼ **Old-fashioned charm** The Hybrid Perpetual rose 'Souvenir du Docteur Jamain' does better against a wall than in the open. It should, however, be sited out of strong sun which can scorch the red-purple, fully double and scented blooms. It associates well with old-fashioned, pale-coloured pinks.

▲ **Californian lilac** The evergreen *Ceanothus impressus* needs sun and wall shelter to see it through the winter months. In late spring, the rigid stems, crowded with small, glossy green leaves, are almost hidden by fluffy clusters of deep blue flowers.

The blue of Californian lilac is successfully set off by an underplanting of miniature *Bellis perennis* 'Pomponette', with double flowers in shades of pink.

▲ **Moroccan broom** With its upright habit and questionable hardiness in northern gardens, the Moroccan broom (*Cytisus battandieri*) is best grown as a wall shrub. Its silver-grey leaves and yellow, cone-shaped flowers in high summer are partnered by *Clematis* 'Etoile Rose', with bell-shaped, cerise flowers, margined silver-pink.

▲ **Partners for walls** The evergreen trumpet honeysuckle (*Lonicera sempervirens*), with brilliant scarlet and orange flowers, is a climbing shrub which needs the support of a wall. Its complementary partner, the dainty, low-growing *Corydalis ochroleuca*, with ferny foliage and creamy flowers, is a common sight in cracks in old walls where it frequently seeds itself.

◄ **Winter shrubs** Most camellias are quite hardy but suffer when exposed to strong winds. They flourish against walls except those facing east, as the morning sun after night frost can ruin the flower buds. *Camellia japonica* 'Adolphe Audusson', with its red, semi-double blooms, is one of the first to flower from late winter onwards. It is handsomely contrasted by the arching branches of elegant *Leucothoë fontanesiana*, also evergreen and intolerant of lime in the soil.

the yellow-brown fruit husks that remain from the insignificant summer flowers split open to reveal the glory of the vine – lustrous scarlet berries set within a golden lining. Be sure to obtain a hermaphrodite plant – one that bears both male and female flowers – otherwise it will not fruit.

Ivies, especially the variegated kinds, are useful in shade, too. The yellow-splashed leaves of *Hedera helix* 'Goldheart' contrast delightfully with the brilliant scarlet flowers of the flame creeper (*Tropaeolum speciosum*), while the white and grey-green foliage of *Hedera canariensis* 'Gloire de Marengo' lightens the autumn colours of Boston ivy (*Parthenocissus tricuspidata*).

Dry-stone walls

Retaining walls and free-standing dry-stone walls make excellent homes for plants requiring sharp drainage – species that, in the wild, colonize steep cliffs and rocky scree slopes. Such plants may have a trailing, tufted, mounded, rosetted, matted or even upright habit.

A sunny wall is ideal for the rosette-forming alpine species. Such groupings could include *Saxifraga cotyledon* 'Southside Seedling' with upright, delicate white and pink blooms. This is a green-leaved species, so introduce contrast with dark red house-leeks such as *Sempervivum* 'Commander Hay'.

For shady walls, small ferns are an obvious choice. To prevent the scene becoming too reminiscent of a dark wood, grow a flowering species such as the 7.5cm (3in) high pink or white fairy foxglove (*Erinus alpinus*) among the ferns.

On tall walls you can afford to grow some of the larger, upright species. Red valerian (*Centranthus ruber*) is excellent for covering a large expanse quickly, though it can look unexciting grown alone. Combine it with *Erigeron mucronatus*, however, and the two will create an enchanting sight, the white tinged pink daisy-like *Erigeron* harmonizing with the valerian.

▲ **Rocky footholds** The little *Campanula portenschlagiana* spills its cascades of violet-blue flowers in sun or shade for most of the summer. It makes a brilliant show against the magenta-pink of *Silene schafta*.

▼ **Dry-stone walls** Many easily grown rockery plants thrive in the minimum of soil. In spring, yellow and golden *Alyssum saxatile* and white candytuft (*Iberis sempervirens*) clothe a wall with colour.

▲ **Wall footing** Small-flowered pansies make excellent partners for alpines. Here, *Viola* 'Jackanapes' lines the foot of a retaining wall planted with pink *Geranium dalmaticum* and deep pink *Dianthus deltoides*.

▲ **Wall companions** A varied company of alpines flourish in the dry soil at the base of a low sunny wall. Tufts of pink and white thrift (*Armeria maritima*) mix their grassy foliage with the succulent leaves of variegated *Sedum kamtschaticum*. The latter sends its sprawling stems over the neat purple rosettes of the common houseleek (*Sempervivum tectorum*).

◄ **Silvery saxifrages** In its native mountain habitat in the Pyrenees, *Saxifraga longifolia* grows on rock faces, producing a single elegant rosette of narrow, silver-encrusted leaves. After several years it displays, in early summer, a 45cm (18in) arching flower plume, glistening white in the form 'Tumbling Waters'. Here, it flows dramatically down a dry-stone wall, frothing over large rosettes of *Sempervivum tectorum* and tiny whorls of purple-tinted *Sedum spathulifolium*.

WATER PLANTS

Garden pools stocked with luxuriant aquatics and moisture-loving marginals are outstanding focal points in spring and summer.

Water brings coolness, serenity and shifting light patterns to the garden. It offers a fascinating canvas for eye-catching associations of water- and moisture-loving plants, many of which are renowned for their exotic flowers and/or striking foliage.

Water lilies (*Nymphaea*), with glossy floating leaf pads and large flowers, are the mainstay of any pool. As a contrast to water lilies, try the floating water hawthorn (*Aponogeton distachyos*) with its large glossy leaves and vanilla-scented waxy white flowers from late spring until autumn. In early summer, the little water violet (*Hottonia palustris*) raises whorls

of pale lilac flowers which are supported by delicate ferny leaves. Water soldier (*Stratiotes aloides*) produces a more dramatic contrast to water lilies, with bold clumps of sword-like leaves that resemble the top of a pineapple.

Use marginal plants, which like to keep their feet wet, in the shallow shelf area of a pool to soften the water's edge. Try bog arum (*Calla palustris*), with 30cm (1ft) high heart-shaped leaves and white-spathed summer flowers, in combination with water forget-me-not (*Myosotis palustris*) and golden club (*Orontium aquaticum*), which has metallic leaves and golden flower spikes. For dra-

matic vertical line effects plant reeds, rushes and water irises, including the many varieties with variegated foliage.

Moisture-loving plants link the water with the rest of the garden. Among the best are feathery astilbe and meadow sweets (*Filipendula rubra* and *F. purpurea*), candelabra primulas with clusters of flowers in spring and early summer, day lilies (*Hemerocallis*),

---

▼ **Poolside plants** The golden marsh marigold (*Caltha palustris* 'Plena') and the massive-leaved skunk cabbage (*Lysichiton americanus*), with its showy yellow flower spadix in spring, thrive in the boggy ground near water.

◄ **Tempered wilderness** The edges of a large pool support a lush vegetation of native plants and moisture-loving perennials. Astilbes, giant cowslips (*Primula florindae*) and shuttlecock ferns (*Matteuccia struthiopteris*) jostle for space alongside a wooden bridge spanning the pool.

rodgersias, bold clumps of hostas, moisture-loving ferns and 1-1.5m (3-5ft) tall purple loosestrife (*Lythrum salicaria*).

Planning a water garden

If the water garden is formal, the regular shape of the pool is all-important, as the plants become decorative features emphasizing its geometrical contours. In an informal pool, however, blurring the boundary between land and water, especially at the edge of a man-made pool, is vital.

In either case, water plants fall into two distinct categories. Firstly, there are true water plants which require water around their roots in order to flourish – from deep-water lilies, golden clubs and water hawthorns to the marginal plants which thrive in shallow water, such as flowering rushes, certain irises, marsh marigolds, arrowheads and bulrushes (*Scirpus*). The so-called oxygenators, which are vital for maintaining the oxygen content of water, are generally quite insignificant in appearance, with the exception of water violet and the water buttercup (*Ranunculus aquatilis*), whose clusters of small, pure white flowers will float on the water surface in late spring.

Secondly, there are moisture-loving plants which grow around the edges of a pool. They prefer moist though not water-logged soil, in sun or light shade, and include astilbes, hostas, day lilies, gunneras, primroses and ferns.

When planting water plants, consider the form, size and leaf colour as well as the flowers – exactly as you would plan associations for herbaceous or mixed borders. The smaller the water feature, the fewer varieties should be used. Select boldly contrasting leaf shapes: flat, round water lily leaves, for example, countered by the sword-like foliage of sweet flag (*Acorus calamus*) or the lacy fairy moss (*Azolla caroliniana*). Choosing several of one carefully

▲ **Bog bean** The aptly named, rhizomatous bog bean (*Menyanthes trifoliata*) is a useful pool plant, growing as happily in deep water as in the muddy ground that surrounds a pool. In early summer, it bears clusters of pinkish-white, fringed flowers which perfectly match the pink plumes of astilbes.

▼ **Marsh marigold** This poolside plant (*Caltha palustris*), also known as kingcup, produces delightful clumps of heart-shaped leaves. In late spring it opens glistening buttercup flowers, their golden rays illuminating tall, red-purple Japanese primroses (*Primula japonica*).

chosen variety, to create a distinct, natural-looking drift, is better than a jumble of individual plants.

Unless you contain plants in special aquatic planting pots and baskets, choose species of roughly equal vigour, otherwise strong growers will soon swamp weaker neighbours. Try to match the size of the pool and surround to the vigour and potential size of a plant. A gunnera, for example, can look exceedingly dramatic near water, but with a height and spread of 3m (10ft), it would be out of scale with a tiny pool.

Some water plants, such as water hyacinth (*Eichhornia crassipes*) and umbrella plant (*Cyperus alternifolius*) need a cool but frost-free spot under cover to over-winter, otherwise they will have to be replaced annually. And some water plants dislike moving water, whether currents in a natural stream or the disturbance caused by an active fountain, tumbling cascade or waterfall.

Year-round interest
A pool and its surround should be attractive in autumn and winter as well as in the growing season. Though most water plants are herbaceous, some, such as sweet flag, are evergreen and fairy moss (*Azolla caroliniana*) turns russet in autumn. If moisture-loving shrubs, such as dogwood (*Cornus*) and willow (*Salix*), are planted near a pool, they can provide winter interest, especially if you choose forms with coloured bark.

With good planning, you can have flowers for most of the year, either in the pool or around it. Marsh marigolds (*Caltha palustris*) and ranunculus – in the pool – and primulas and globe flowers (*Trollius*) – around the margins – blossom throughout the spring months; water forget-me-nots (*Myosotis palustris*), mimulus and water lilies (*Nymphaea*) fill the pool with summer colour; and water hawthorn (*Aponogeton distachyos*) and reedmace (*Typha*) flower in autumn. For fragrance, there are the aromatic leaves of water mint (*Mentha aquatica*) and sweet flag – the labiate mint flowers also attract insects.

A pool and its planting should form a complete 'picture' in itself as well as being part of the larger garden scene. Use the planting, both in and around the pool, to

◄ **Water lilies** With their beautiful cup-shaped flowers and broad green leaf pads, water lilies (*Nymphaea*) are the most popular of all water plants. They also provide cover and shade for ornamental fish.

► **Foliage contrasts** Wide clumps of hostas on the pool surround ease the transition from still water to hard paving.

▼ **Streamside banks** Densely planted with water irises and native ferns, a stream integrates naturally into the overall garden picture.

reinforce an existing colour scheme, or liven it up with exciting new contrasts. Most native British water plants have white, yellow or blue flowers, which make a restful combination. Water lilies and other exotic plants come in pinks, oranges, reds and purples, and create a vivid, vibrant effect.

Balancing water plants

Many water plants serve useful purposes as well as being attractive. They help to create an ecological balance that is vital in still water, especially in small, man-made pools without recirculating pumps. The oxygenators are the most important, but submerged, floating aquatics, moisture-lovers, deep marginal plants and even water lilies all play a part.

Oxygenators help to keep the water clear and 'sweet'. They provide oxygen for fish and other livestock, and somewhere for fish to lay their eggs, as well as assimilating the carbon dioxide given off by fish during respiration. These plants maintain the correct oxygen content of the water and spend all or most of their lives submerged, though some, such as water violet (*Hottonia palustris*) and water crowfoot (*Ranunculus aquatilis*), rise to the surface to flower. Many have delicate, ferny foliage, so that water can flow through them without damage.

If there is a layer of soil on the pool bottom, planting is easy. Simply tie a small weight or stone to the cut ends of a clump of oxygenators, and lower it into the water. Otherwise, plant in a small clay flower pot filled with loam-based compost. Some oxygenators – Canadian pondweed (*Elodea canadensis*), for example – can become invasive. Hook out any excess with a rake – it makes excellent compost.

Floaters are usually small and, except for water soldier (*Stratiotes aloides*), frogbit (*Hydrocharis morsus-ranae*), and the invasive duckweed (*Lemna*), tender. Floating plants are not anchored, so they drift and re-assemble in response to water currents, wind or even the movement of fish.

Floaters provide food for fish and shade the water, which helps to keep algae down. The long, trailing roots of frogbit and water hyacinth (*Eichhornia crassipes*) offer hiding places for fish fry and

▲ **Water meadow** In high summer, a narrow stream coursing through a meadow of grass and wild plants is edged by twin ranks of *Primula helodoxa*. The bright golden-yellow candelabra heads are borne atop 90cm (3ft) tall stems rising from shiny evergreen leaf rosettes.

▲ **Moisture lovers** By late spring, the bog primula (*Primula florindae*) is in full, scented bloom, raising its heads of cowslip-like yellow bells on white-dusted stems up to 90cm (3ft) tall. The yellow theme continues with glossy-leaved monkey musk (*Mimulus luteus*) partnered by elegant blue Jacob's ladder (*Polemonium caeruleum*).

▼ **Summer marginals** Sheltered by sword-shaped, variegated iris foliage, near-hardy ground orchids (*Dactylorrhiza elata*) push up their dense spikes of purple flowers in early summer. The colour is repeated in purple-pink *Primula japonica*, nodding above the large, heart-shaped leaves of *Caltha palustris*.

▲ **Pool planting** The clean lines of a formal pool should never be obscured. Highlight its geometrical shape with one or two corner clumps of shallow-water acorus or irises, with water lilies occupying much of the centre.

water insects. To plant, simply place them on the surface of the water. Some, such as fairy moss and frogbit, form winter buds or turons, which sink to the bottom of the pool in autumn and rise again the following spring.

Water lilies, with their exotic flowers, are the most popular water plants. Their leaves serve a practical purpose, sheltering fish, shading the water and preventing the growth of algae.

There are hundreds of varieties available, most of which are hardy and bloom during daylight. Leaf and flower size range from miniatures to giants with blooms and leaf pads as large as dinner plates. Hardy water lilies vary in colour from pure white to pink, red, yellow, orange and copper, many changing to darker shades on successive days. Tender or tropical water lilies are also available for

planting in early summer in shallow warm water, or in indoor heated pools; some of these are night-blooming, and their flamboyant flowers, often with crimped or frilled edges, come in more exotic colours that include blue and purple.

Some water lilies require water up to 90cm (3ft) deep while others will flourish in shallow pools and even tubs with a surface area of 60cm (2ft). Make sure you choose a type that matches the space and depth available. A pool entirely covered with rampant water lily pads is ecologically unsound as well as unattractive. (As a general rule, ⅓ to ½ of the water surface should be covered by plants.)

In natural pools, water lilies can be lowered into the water between sods of turf, but it is easier to control them if they are planted in aquatic perforated baskets.

Deep-water aquatics are alternatives to water lilies, and are planted in much the same way. They include the white water hawthorn (*Aponogeton distachyos*), with its long flowering period and attractive boat-shaped leaves, and the yellow-flowered water fringe (*Nymphoides peltata*).

Marginals are by far the largest category. Marginal plants such as sweet flag, marsh marigold and forget-me-not need either shallow water or continually moist soil, although some marginals are happy in both. Marginals are less essential ecologically than oxygenators, though the mini-jungle created by their roots and stems offers good hiding places for young fish and, as with other water plants, they use up minerals in the water and keep down algae.

Poolside plants

This large category encompasses a range of species, from those that qualify as marginals to ordinary border plants, such as hostas, astilbes and globe flowers that like, but don't actually need, moisture at the roots. Most true bog plants prefer damp rather than wet soil.

In man-made pools the water is contained by a liner or concrete shell, so the adjacent soil may well be bone dry. For a bog-garden effect with a smooth, gradual transition between water and land, choose such moisture-lovers as *Iris sibirica*, hostas, primulas or loosestrife.

◄ **Waterside companions** The orange-red, daisy-like flowers of *Ligularia dentata* 'Desdemona' are instantly eye-catching, though the lustrous deep green leaves backed with bright purple are equally spectacular. This moisture-loving perennial demands bold partners – large-leaved skunk cabbage (*Lysichiton americanus*), purple loosestrife (*Lythrum salicaria*) and royal fern (*Osmunda regalis*).

► **Marginal plants** Where a rock garden slopes down to an informal pool, the moist pockets of soil which form are ideal for the incomparable hostas. Magnificent in their diversity of leaf shape and colour, from bluish-green to lime-yellow, they fit naturally into pool plantings. Their rounded shapes are contrasted by upright, purple *Iris laevigata*.

▼ **Cotton grass** Ideal for shallow water and bog gardens, the elegant cotton grass (*Eriophorum angustifolium*) makes an unusual partner for the golden-flowered marsh marigold (*Caltha palustris*). The cotton-wool tufts of white flowers introduce a cool element to the pool's lily pads and, on the far side, the vertical clumps of sweet flag (*Acorus calamus*).

▲ **Miniature pools** Waterproof tubs and barrels make excellent miniature water features for a patio. They can be planted with small water lilies and, as here, with the unusual, non-flowering water horsetail (*Equisetum*).

◄ **Water hawthorn** As well as its distinctively long floating leaves, the water hawthorn (*Aponogeton distachyos*) bears clusters of sweetly scented, pure white flowers in summer.

▼ **Informal pools** Small pools need careful planting. Introduce deep and shallow-water plants that don't crowd the surface. Light and air are crucial to maintaining an ecological balance.

MOVING WATER

**The sound and sight of moving water bring life
and sparkle to a garden – and there are delightful water
features for even the smallest space.**

Moving water is an endless source of attraction, as it constantly changes in appearance according to the light, the weather and its surroundings. Besides pleasing the eye and the ear, it can also evoke feelings of reverie and peacefulness.

In a large garden the sound of moving water stirs interest long before the source itself is visible, while in a smaller garden moving water automatically becomes a focal point.

In practical terms, the movement adds oxygen to the water, so any fish benefit. The spray from a fountain also helps cleanse the water's surface by sinking dust.

Few gardens are blessed with natural moving water, but it's easy to install a fountain or water course. Many such features come in kit form, and purpose-built fixtures widen the range of options even more.

Waterfalls and cascades involve water dropping from higher to lower levels. A waterfall is a continuous drop, while a cascade is a series of smaller, connected waterfalls or steep channels, often with pools between. Both come as preformed, rigid plastic or glassfibre moulds, and flexible liners.

Fountains are jets of spouting or bubbling water, and can be freestanding or wall mounted.

Purpose-built features

You can make your own fountain by connecting a water supply to any weather-proof, water-proof container, such as an urn, old copper washing bowl, stone sink or half-barrel. Artificial streams can be constructed from natural stone or waterproofed concrete.

On a larger scale, such projects are best undertaken with the help of professional advice and contractors. If any natural water is

▶ **Natural streams** Moisture-loving marginals emphasize the winding course of a natural stream. Swathes of golden monkey musks (*Mimulus luteus*) catch the bright light and are reflected in the water.

▲ **Animal-shaped fountain** Fish, herons, dolphins, seals, sea lions and frogs are popular as water fountains. They can be mounted on display pedestals, of natural or reconstituted stone, for greater visual impact.

▼ **Contemporary style** A group of polished stainless steel mushroom sprays of differing heights creates an impressive focal point. Tall fountains should be sited so that strong winds won't blow the water off course.

▲ **Traditional feature** Available in a variety of different guises, standard pool fountains usually represent mythological creatures or classical figures. A boy bearing a scalloped bowl is a popular and typical choice.

Pool fountains can be made of stone, reconstituted stone, lead, bronze, copper, terracotta, plastic or glassfibre, and vary in price according to material, size and style.

Fountains installed in pools containing water lilies and ornamental fish should be restricted to a small, softly playing jet of water.

► ▲ **Millstone fountain** Original or reproduction millstones make attractive water features in small gardens. They are easy to install, at or above ground level, with a concealed pump bubbling water through the central hole and over the sides.

► **Pool-side spout** As an alternative to pool fountains, ornamental water jets can be fixed to the sides of a pool. Traditional models include little urchins urinating or mermaids emptying urns of water.

▲ **Miniature waterfall** Water recirculated from a pump in a raised pool trickles through a pipe into a narrow water course on a lower level.

diverted, the approval of the local water board and planning authority may be needed.

Shapes and sizes

Water features and the mechanical apparatus needed to operate them can be quite expensive, so cost is a prime consideration although other factors play a part.

In small gardens, small-scale water features are best. Wall-mounted fountains or self-contained patio fountains are particularly suitable. Buy good-quality fixtures, since they will all be viewed at close range. In larger gardens, size depends on location. A fountain in the middle of a lawn should be large enough to command attention.

Waterfalls and cascades need slopes or vertical level changes. Few gardens have these naturally, but a common solution for

level gardens is to use the soil dug out during the construction of a pool to build an adjacent rockery, down which water can fall or tumble.

A fountain looks best in a formal pool, while a waterfall or cascade is usually better in a natural-looking pool. A waterfall connecting formal pools on two levels can be successful, provided it does not pretend to be natural; so can formal, step-like cascades.

Neither fish nor water lilies survive long in a small pool with a vigorous fountain, although a single small jet, used occasionally, does no harm.

Water courses made from concrete or sheet liner systems look more natural if they are kept fairly narrow and winding. The natural effect can be enhanced by covering the base of the course with dark-coloured shingle or rounded pebbles and placing larger stones here and there to create ripples in the water.

If you are adding a fountain, waterfall or cascade to an existing

pool, the location is relatively fixed. If starting from scratch, try to site the water feature where it will get some sun, since moving water is most effective when it catches the light.

You need a nearby electrical outlet from which to run the pump. Ideally, the cable should be buried or otherwise concealed.

Site a fountain in a sheltered spot, where strong winds won't blow the spray off course. For the same reason, it shouldn't be too close to a path.

Waterfalls and cascades

These can be quite small and still effective – even a drop of 15cm (6in) is enough. The smaller the amount of water circulating, though, the narrower the waterfall head should be, to get the maximum effect. Many designs have centre-pouring 'lips' for small flows of water.

Preformed moulds of rigid plastic or more expensive glassfibre are quick and easy to install. They can look quite natural, but you are limited to the shapes, sizes and colours available.

You can also use waterproof sheet liner systems for the water courses. Made of polythene, butyl, or specially reinforced PVC, these come in a range of sizes – if necessary, two liners can be joined together with special waterproof tape or by vulcanizing. Life expectancies range from five to fifty years, with prices and guarantees to match.

Liners are more difficult to install than rigid moulds, and may require special polyester matting if the ground beneath is particularly stony. Design possibilities are wider, though, and if the edges are concealed, a more natural-looking result is possible.

Concrete water courses are rarely made nowadays, because of the cost, the skilled labour needed, and the risk of cracking with age or from frost. However, a concrete or carved Portland stone ledge with water spilling over it is an attractive possibility.

Pool fountains

The simplest fountains consist of a jet installed in a pool. The spray can be predetermined and is usually created by a submersible pump, the power of which also determines the height that the spray will reach.

Spray heads of polished stainless steel, brass, terracotta and plastic are available. Most single jets have only one spray pattern, such as a geyser, plume or revolving arc. A 'water bell' jet produces a bell-shaped spray, and there are also single and multiple 'water bell' jets.

Some jets have interchangeable heads, each one producing a different spray pattern. Others provide a repeating series of spray patterns, with several changes per minute. There are also jets which mix air with water to produce a foaming plume.

Some jets have optical lighting systems, which illuminate the fountain from below. Single colour systems are the most restful, and white lights are the most natural.

Traditional pool fountains often represent mythological creatures

◄ **Imitating nature** A large rock garden incorporates a waterfall flowing over flat stones. The edges of the water course are lushly planted with moisture-loving hostas, ferns and astilbes, and tall, purple-flowered *Iris sibirica*.

▼ **Split-level pools** Three interconnected raised pools create a fascinating water feature. A fountain in the centre pool adds sound and movement without disturbing the fish in the upper pool.

▲ **Small-scale water features** Any frostproof container large enough to contain a pump can be made into an attractive water feature. Here, a terracotta urn softly spilling water adds a Mediterranean touch to the brick surround of a raised pool.

▶ **Oriental water spout** A secluded corner of a garden can become a haven of peace and tranquillity with the introduction of a simple water feature. A bamboo water spout trickles a flow of water into a miniature basin set between rocks.

or classical figures. Variations include Peter Pan, idealized rural characters – country lads and lasses – and water cherubs either singly or in clusters.

Animal-shaped pool fountains come in the form of dolphins, frogs, seals, sea lions, fish and herons. Simple and ornate basins, scallop shells and bowls shaped like flowers or overlapping lotus leaves are available fitted with jets. Some manufacturers offer optional pedestals, for greater height and visual impact.

Self-contained fountains

If you don't have a pool, but would still like a fountain, opt for one of the self-contained units which have a collection basin either at the top – rather like a drinking fountain or bird bath – or at the base. They need very little water and only a small pump and so can be situated almost anywhere in

the garden or patio where the sound of water is always soothing.

Designs range from the simple to the ornate, and from the modern to the classical. In some cases, statues and bowls can be bought separately, to give a wider choice.

Wall fountains

Millstone or bubble fountains are inspired by natural springs, and usually consist of a round, flat stone from which a gentle, central flow of water emerges. The even film of water trickling over the stone surface enhances its beauty.

Original millstones can be quite expensive and difficult to find, but reproduction millstones made of reconstituted stone or sand-coated glassfibre are readily available. They are simply fitted over a

shallow water tank and flexible plastic sheeting, which collects the water. They can be displayed at ground level, or higher, depending on whether the water tank is buried. The plastic sheeting can be covered with a layer of smooth, dark-coloured cobbles or pebbles.

Wall-fountains are space saving and include classical dolphins, lion masks and gargoyles with water spouting from their mouths. They are usually set in plaques, for easy mounting, and displayed with a semicircular collection bowl underneath. The bowls can be simple or ornate, and large or small, depending on available space and the size of the flow. A wall fountain could also empty directly into a pool.

Scented partners

Fragrance is elusive and intangible – it is sometimes delicate and sometimes cloying. We instinctively seek the scent of flowers of exquisite shape and colour, but are often disappointed. In their quest for perfect colour and form, plant breeders have largely sacrificed scent. So, in order to recapture a perfumed garden, we often have to revert to old-fashioned flower species.

Many blooms have unforgettable scents – the sweet fragrance of jonquil narcissi, the heady scent of lilac after rain, the spicy aroma of old-fashioned roses and certain lilies, and the unexpected, almost overpowering fragrance of *Viburnum farreri* in late autumn. Generally, they are most noticeable on warm summer evenings when the essential flower oils are released into the air.

As each scent tends to be distinctive, it is best not to mix them. Delicate rose fragrances should not have to compete with strongly redolent honeysuckles, nor sweet lavender with clove-scented pinks.

Aromatic foliage, notably that of herbs, is less overt than flower perfumes and usually has to be bruised or pinched to release their aromas. Sprigs of rosemary or bay are perfect for a barbecue, unlike the pungent smell of rue and the aniseed scent of fennel which always linger in their immediate surroundings.

Perfumed plants should ideally be grown where they can be readily encountered: scented climbers and wall shrubs by house windows and doors, or trained on pillars and arbours near a patio. Grow fragrant nicotianas, wallflowers and old-fashioned pinks close to a path, hyacinths and scented stock in window boxes, and verbenas in hanging baskets.

Fragrant roses The scent of golden-yellow climbing 'Goldfinch' mingles with that of scarlet 'Souvenir de Claudius Denoyel'.

FRAGRANT ROSES

**The majestic rose has endured for
thousands of years, loved for its perfect form,
pure colours and exquisite fragrance.**

It is often said that modern roses have little or no fragrance. It is true that in many cases plant breeders, in their quest for perfection of form, clarity of colour and continuity of bloom, have produced roses where scent is at best elusive. However, many of the modern roses – bush, shrub and climbers – are as outstanding for their fragrance as for their flower shape and colours.

All scented roses should be sited where their fragrance can waft across the garden or through open windows. Ideally, they should be placed in a sunny position which also receives light shade. In bright sun, wine-red 'Souvenir du Docteur Jamain', for example, will suffer sun-scorch and a reduction in its strong fragrance.

Modern bush roses
The large-flowered bush roses, better known as hybrid tea, are possibly the best loved of all roses. They are popular for their double-flowered, shapely blooms on sturdy stems and for their long flowering season. They are perfect as cut flowers, especially those with exquisite fragrance, such as the long-established 'Alec's Red', the coral-pink 'Blessings', and the yellow-orange 'Sutter's Gold'. One of the most strongly scented is the crimson-scarlet 'Ena Harkness'. Sadly, its velvety flowers droop from weak stems, unlike that fine bedding rose 'Fragrant Cloud' whose dusky red, shapely buds open to coral-salmon; the scent is exceptionally potent in the autumn flush.

Cluster-flowered bush roses or floribundas differ little from the large-flowered roses, except that the single, semi-double or double flowers are borne in large clusters on more branching and vigorous bushes. Scented varieties include the golden-yellow 'Arthur Bell', the salmon-pink 'Dearest' and the orange-vermilion 'Matangi'. The vigorous 'Chinatown', 1.5m (5ft) tall, has deliciously scented, pink-tinted flowers while 'Escapade' smells of musk and the white 'Margaret Merril', tinged pink,

▼ **Bed of roses** The scent of climbing and rambling roses rises high above pink and dusky red modern bush roses. Sweet-smelling lavender is a traditional partner to roses, in the garden and in pot-pourri.

is the most heavily scented of all the floribundas.

Shrub and climbing roses

Like the old roses, from which shrub roses have been bred, these are less formal in habit than bush roses and belong in shrub and mixed borders or as specimen plants. They differ from their ancestors in being largely repeat-flowering from early summer through to autumn, bearing their blooms singly or in small clusters. Although they lack the autumn colours and bright hips of old roses, a few are scented and are perfect for siting as specimen shrubs near sitting areas. Choose between that old favourite, the pink 'Constance Spry' with a heavy scent of myrrh, and the carmine, deeply fragrant 'Kathleen Ferrier', the pure white 'Jacqueline du Pré' or 'Lavender Lassie'.

The 'New English Shrub Roses' combine the colour range and repeat-flowering behaviour of modern shrub roses with the form and heady fragrance of old roses.

Repeat-flowering modern climbers include several fragrant varieties. They are ideal for training over pergolas and arbours or up pillars; the more vigorous types are perfect for climbing up tall house walls and trees. The following are notable for their scent: 'Compassion' (salmon-pink and orange), 'Dreaming Spires' (golden-yellow), 'Schoolgirl' (orange-apricot) and 'Souvenir de Claudius Denoyel' (crimson).

Old roses

In the fifth century BC, Heroditus, the Greek 'father of history', described a rose with sixty petals whose scent was more overpowering than any other. It might possibly be *Rosa damascena*, whose scent has been described as being 'neither heady nor too strong, not stuffing or unpleasant sweet'. The oil distilled from its petals were used in the commercial production of perfumes and rose water. (On

◀ **Modern scents** Bush roses, better known as floribundas and hybrid teas, are exquisite in form though less fragrant than their ancestors. Some, however, such as 'Fragrant Cloud' (*background*) are heavily scented, especially in autumn. The scarlet 'Lilli Marlene' (*foreground*) and the vigorous, clear pink 'Queen Elizabeth' have a more delicate scent.

the other side of the world, the Chinese also cultivated roses on a massive scale, among them highly fragrant varieties. They, too, were used for distilling rose oil and water, but here such luxuries were reserved exclusively for emperors and the nobility.)

Many of the old roses deserve a place in the modern garden. Although most flower only once in the season, in early and high summer, they are exquisite in form and fragrance, usually with attractive foliage in autumn and splendid hips in late summer. They are also more resistant to pests and diseases than modern roses.

Species roses are the ancestors of modern roses and closely resemble wild roses. Chiefly distinctive for their foliage, strong prickles and outstanding hips, they are valuable in the wild garden or as specimen shrubs. The sweetbriar (*R. rubinosa*, syn. *R. eglantaria*) resembles the dog rose, except that its foliage is covered with glands that emit an apple fragrance on warm summer evenings. The Scotch rose (*R. spinosissima*) is a suckering, remontant shrub with richly scented, pale pink blooms that fade to white.

Species roses produced a number of hybrids and sports, either naturally or through cross-breeding, and these so-called old-fashioned roses were widely grown until the introduction of the Hybrid Teas in the 19th century. Many were heavily scented, and several have survived to perfume modern gardens.

Alba roses are strong-growing shrubs, 1.8m (6ft) or more tall, with finely toothed leaves and a mass of large, pale-coloured blooms, sweetly scented and often quartered in shape. Among the best and most readily available are 'Celestial' ('Céleste'), with soft pink, semi-double blooms; the more fragrant 'Great Maiden's Blush', a survivor from the 15th century with full-petalled, blush-pink flowers, and 'Königin von Dänemarck' with quartered pale pink blooms.

Bourbon roses are crosses between Damask and China roses which have inherited the intense fragrance of the former and the repeat-flowering habit of the latter. The huge, full-petalled and quartered flowers are borne on spreading shrubs about 1.8 (6ft) tall, with a profusion of deliciously scented flowers, purple-pink in 'Mme Isaac Pereire' and white and crimson-budded in 'Boule de Neige'.

Cabbage roses, also known as Provence roses, are derived from *R. centifolia* and although more compact in habit (up to 1.8m/6ft tall), they usually need support for the floppy, thorny stems. Clusters of deeply fragrant, double and flat-topped flowers are borne in high summer. 'Fantin Latour', pale pink shaded with deeper blushes, and 'Rose de Meaux', a dwarf shrub with small, bright pink blooms, are among the best.

Damask roses are the most fragrant of all types. Their 7.5cm (3in) wide double flowers, often with incurved centres, are shaded from dark pink to white. They are borne in loose clusters in early and high summer and are followed by slender and hairy hips. Outstanding varieties include grey-leaved and pink-flowered 'Celsiana', the darker pink, richly scented 'Gloire de Guilan' and the pure white, green-eyed 'Mme Hardy'.

Gallica roses are the oldest and largest group of the old roses. They thrive in poor soil but will not tolerate shade. They grow 1.2-1.5m (4-5ft) high, with double, richly scented flowers in high summer. 'Belle de Crécy' is of lax habit and may need support for its thornless stems set with purple-red flowers that mature to violet. 'Rosa Mundi', the old and well-known striped rose ('Versicolor'), is conspicuously red and white, while 'Tuscany Superb' is notable for its velvety, golden-centred purple blooms.

Hybrid musk roses are bushy and spreading and are distinctive for the small, deliciously scented flowers borne in large clusters from late summer until the autumn frosts. The apricot-yellow 'Buff Beauty' with a tea-like fragrance is one of the finest; 'Penelope', 1.5m (5ft) tall, has broad glossy foliage and musk-scented blooms of flushed apricot that fades to pale yellow.

Moss roses were the mainstay of Victorian rose gardens and much loved for their deeply fragrant summer blooms. They are characterized by resin-scented mossy glands on the sepals, and by their bristly stems. 'Nuits de Young' bears small velvety flowers of deep maroon-purple with prominent golden centres. 'William Lobb', an ideal pillar rose, is crimson fading to lavender.

Rugosa roses are among the most popular of the old roses and widely used for hedging and as specimen shrubs. They are ultra-hardy and vigorous, with prickly stems and wrinkled leaves that turn yellow in autumn among large orange-red hips. The single or double flowers are borne mainly in high summer but continue sporadically until early autumn. The large, bowl-shaped blooms are heavily scented.

Popular, readily available varieties include the double, yellow-flowered 'Agnes', the magnificent white 'Blanc Double de Coubert', and the pale pink 'Fru Dagmar Hastrup'. The double, crimson-flowered 'Roseraie de l'Hay' has a scent like sugared almonds and flowers almost continuously.

▼ **Arctic sea** The glistening white, rounded forms of 'Iceberg' roses rise from unruffled waves of fragrant lavender. A background of purple *Lavandula* 'Grappenhall' merges into the darker coloured 'Hidcote', capped by a white foam of snow-in-summer (*Cerastium tomentosum*).

PERFUMED PLANTS

**Scented flowers and aromatic foliage create
visual and sensual delights, most appreciable in sunny
and sheltered corners of beds and borders.**

Many flowers have evolved bold colours, special shapes and nectar to attract pollinating insects, and some have also developed a scent to make themselves attractive.

Leaves, too, can be scented – although this is sometimes not apparent until they have been pinched, bruised or even crushed – particularly herbs and the leaves of shrubs from the Mediterranean or areas with a similar climate. Here, the scent comes from the release of volatile oils, which have been evolved to reduce water loss and to deter grazing animals.

The biggest and brightest flowers are not always the most fragrant – in fact, it is often the smaller, usually insignificant, flowers which smell most strongly. In the quest for larger and more flamboyant blooms, plant breeders have overlooked scent, to the extent that many plants have lost the fragrance they once had as wild species. For example, roses, carnations and sweet peas don't always have the scent you remember and expect.

Generally, scents are stronger during hot sunny days than on cold dull ones – this is particularly true of shrubs with aromatic leaves which release their oils in such conditions. Even winter-scented flowers are more fragrant during milder spells. Roses, honeysuckles, jasmine, lilacs and stocks smell best after rain.

Fragrant plants include annuals, biennials, perennials, bulbs, shrubs or climbers – so sweet-smelling plants can be sited practically anywhere in the garden – on a patio or above a door or window, for instance.

Patio plants

The gaps between the paving stones of a patio make an ideal site for a small group of plants whose leaves must be crushed to release their scent. They can be gently walked upon, but will not stand up to constant trampling.

Several small perennials are also suitable. The dense, mat-forming varieties of thyme (*Thymus serpyllum*) need full sun and revel in the warmth reflected from stone. In spring and summer, the prostrate Corsican mint (*Mentha requienii*) is studded with tiny lavender-coloured flowers, and its leaves smell strongly of peppermint. Blooming later and larger in size, pennyroyal (*Mentha pulegium*) is extremely minty. Variegated ground ivy (*Nepeta hederacea* 'Variegata'), too, is pleasantly minty. The common chamomile (*Anthemis nobilis*), in its non-flowering form 'Treneague', is a fragrant grass substitute. Yellow stonecrop (*Sedum acre*) spreads rapidly while thrift forms neat, small hummocks.

▼ **Lilac season** Late spring and early summer arrive with the heady fragrance of lilac (*Syringa*). The dense, upright panicles range in colour from white and yellow to blue, red and purple.

folium and the evergreen *L. japon-ica* 'Halliana' are scented.

Another old-fashioned sweetly scented climber is white-flowered summer jasmine (*Jasminum offi-cinale*) which, like honeysuckle, smells much stronger during the evening.

Climbing roses enhance any doorway and some of the most fragrant include the velvety 'Crimson Glory', yellow 'Rêve d'Or' and cérise-pink 'Zéphirine Drouhin'.

Other suitable climbers include the Virgin's bower (*Clematis flammula*), with its strongly fragrant little flowers, and the Moroccan broom (*Cytisus battandieri*), which has pineapple-scented flowers and silvery leaves.

Edging plants
Plant aromatic-leaved plants alongside a sunny path to be

Container plants
A container of fragrant plants can brighten up and scent any corner of the garden – from a box under a window to a pot on a patio. One advantage is that you can site the container where the scent can best be appreciated.

Suitable plants for containers include wallflowers, sweet Williams, primroses, polyanthus and, later in the year, petunias, Virginia and night-scented stock, reseda and nicotianas. Hyacinths are also beautifully fragrant, as are some of the lilies, such as *Lilium regale, L. speciosum, L. auratum* and *L. formosanum.*

A tub of pelargoniums has a distinctive smell, more noticeable after watering. Surround this with pots of scented-leaf varieties, which have unimpressive flowers but attractively shaped and often variegated leaves (these release strong scents when pinched). *Pelargonium crispum* 'Variegatum', for example, is lemon-scented, and others smell of peppermint, orange, chocolate, nutmeg or apples.

Framing doors and windows
Door and window surrounds are perfect places for training fragrant climbing plants, so that their scents are wafted into the house, or enjoyed as you pass by.

Sweetly scented climbers such as the honeysuckles spring to mind although, surprisingly, not all honeysuckles are fragrant. *Lonicera periclymenum, L. capri-*

▲ **Sweet scent** Flowering in mid-spring, the Chinese *Osmanthus delavayi* is a slow-growing evergreen with sweetly-scented, jasmine-like white flowers. It does well in sun or light shade, sheltered from cold winds.

▼ **Fragrant woodbine** The common honeysuckle or woodbine (*Lonicera periclymenum*) bears clusters of fragrant creamy-white and red blooms. Flowering from early summer on, it thrives on walls of any aspect.

▲ **Perfumed wall companions** Time and patience are amply rewarded with a magnificent late-spring association of *Wisteria sinensis* and *Rosa banksiae* 'Lutea'. On a vast sunny wall, pale mauve, vanilla-scented wisteria tassels mingle with the near-evergreen yellow rose whose delicately fragranced blooms resemble double primroses.

▶ **Evening scent** The sweet-smelling tobacco plant (*Nicotiana*) blooms unceasingly throughout summer. Most modern varieties open their flowers during the day, but the scent is most powerful at night, especially in the white-flowered form 'Fragrant Cloud'.

◀ **Night-scented stocks** All stocks are fragrant, but the night-scented stock (*Matthiola bicornis*), a hardy annual, has a more intoxicating sweetness than any other. The evening air is scented in late summer with the heady perfumes of white-flowered nicotianas and delicate pink-flowered night stock. Clumps of sweet William (*Dianthus barbatus* 'Giant White') and red-tinged mignonettes (*Reseda odorata*) provide strong daytime fragrances.

► **Scent of roses** The large-flowered, hybrid tea rose 'Grandpa Dickson' is a sturdy, dark-leaved rose with an abundance of yellow flowers in summer and autumn. Their light fragrance is augmented by strongly perfumed tobacco plants (*Nicotiana alata* 'Lime Green'), which form a vivid contrast to purple-leaved *Berberis thunbergii* 'Atropurpurea'.

▲ **Flowering hedge** The Persian lilac (*Syringa × persica* 'Alba') forms a rounded shrub smothered in late spring with panicles of scented white flowers. Their spicy perfume almost overwhelms the fragrance of its companion, the pink and lilac broom (*Cytisus* 'Zeelandia').

◄ **Mock orange** The rich orange-like fragrance of *Philadelphus microphyllus* fills the air around an early-summer composition in white. The small-leaved branches of mock orange, festooned with white flowers, arch down to greet the blossom of evergreen *Escallonia* 'Iveyi' and the bell-shaped flowers of *Campanula alliariifolia*.

brushed against as you pass. The fragrances released by lavender, rosemary, cotton lavender, southernwood (*Artemisia abrotanum*) and rue, particularly on a hot day, are reminiscent of the scented scrublands of the Mediterranean.

If the path passes along the base of a retaining wall, take the opportunity of growing scented plants along the top of it. Suitable varieties include catmint, sweet alyssum, pinks, golden-leaved marjoram and the larger kinds of thyme, such as *Thymus × citriodorus* and *T. vulgaris*.

Border plants

There are few scented plants among 'standard' perennials, but *Phlox paniculata* is one – the white and mauve varieties are the best. Bergamot (*Monarda didyma*) has red, pink or purple hooded flowers in whorls; the whole plant is aromatic, as is the burning bush (*Dictamnus albus*).

In late spring, sweetly scented lilies-of-the-valley (*Convallaria majalis*) bloom, followed by lupins, pinks and garden carnations. In high summer, exotic lilies mingle with roses and later with fragrant chrysanthemums.

Scented annuals and bedding plants such as wallflowers, sweet Williams and primroses can be included in borders with sweet peas, perhaps trained along the border fence, for summer fragrance. There are mignonettes (*Reseda odorata*), the various stocks with clove-like scents, cherry pie (*Heliotropium arborescens*), whose common name describes its scent, and the hybrid verbenas, though the red ones are scentless.

Spring and summer scents

Few shrubs can surpass the daphnes for exquisite scent, beginning with *D. mezereum* whose purple-pink flowers wreathe the leafless branches from late winter on. The dwarf evergreen garland flower (*D. cneorum*) and the spicy-scented *D. × burkwoodii*, both rose-pink, follow in late spring and early summer.

Azara microphylla, a small evergreen tree with yellow vanilla-scented flowers, provides one of the first scents of spring. Also evergreen, *Osmanthus delavayi* has profuse white, almost jasmine-like flowers in mid-spring. The yellow azalea (*Rhododendron luteum*) is extremely fragrant.

▲ **Honey-scented azalea** The deciduous azalea (*Rhododendron luteum*) bears large clusters of fragrant, yellow trumpets in late spring. As an added bonus, the leaves take on orange, scarlet and purple tints in autumn.

▶ **Summer scents** On hot, still summer days the combined fragrances of mock orange (*Philadelphus*) and cottage-garden lavender are reminiscent of scented Mediterranean scrublands.

▼ **Thyme cover** The mat-forming species of thyme (*Thymus serpyllum*) make delightfully fragrant carpets. They will creep over rock gardens, raised beds and among paving cracks, releasing a strong aroma from their leaves, though the flowers are also scented.

▲ Window frames The sweet-scented climbing rose 'Zéphyiine Drouhin' is perfect for framing windows and doors. Its cerise-pink, semi-double flowers are particularly fragrant in autumn.

▼ Sweet mignonette This hardy annual (*Reseda odorata*) is a popular cottage-garden plant, prized by bees for its yellow, white and orange flower heads, tinged red in some varieties.

Lilacs, which begin to bloom in late spring, have a heady fragrance and there are numerous colours to choose from. The white summer flowers of mock orange (*Philadelphus*) fill the air with their all-pervading scent.

For late summer scent, honey-scented *Buddleia davidii* and two members of the pea family with panicles of golden yellow flowers are particularly good – the Mount Etna broom (*Genista aetnensis*) and the Spanish broom (*Spartium junceum*).

Winter scents
Many winter-flowering plants carry perfumes, a high percentage of them being shrubs. Plant them near a path where they can be easily enjoyed.

Among the deciduous shrubs which bear flowers uncluttered by leaves is the Chinese witch hazel (*Hamamelis mollis*). Its penetrating scent comes from clusters of yellow spider-like flowers in early and mid-winter.

Better with the protection of a wall, the wintersweet (*Chimonanthus praecox*) needs several years before it produces its small, waxy, purple-centred yellowish flowers. *Viburnum×bodnantense*, on the other hand, reaches flowering size in a few years, when it bears clusters of rose-pink blooms that scent the air in autumn and winter.

Happy in shade, the evergreen mahonias, *Mahonia japonica* and *Mahonia* 'Charity', carry sprays of yellow blooms scented like lily-of-the-valley all winter.

Iris reticulata and *I. unguicularis* are delicately fragrant. The former is for the rock garden or for pots on the patio in late winter, while the latter needs poor soil and all the sun it can get.

Night scents
Several plants give off their strongest scent at dusk and later in the night. Often, they have pale, tubular flowers.

This group includes some lilies, honeysuckles, *Hosta plantaginea* and the flowering tobacco plant (*Nicotiana alata*), in its pale, tall forms and the even taller, white-flowered *Nicotiana sylvestris*. In the same family, angel's trumpet (*Datura suaveolens*), a tender shrub with large drooping flowers, would scent a patio if planted in a large pot.

The common names of night-

▲ **Regal splendour** The glorious white trumpets of *Lilium regale* waft their spicy fragrance above a clump of aromatic *A. maritima* 'Powys Castle', with silvery filigree foliage. Good colour contrast is provided by purple orach (*Atriplex hortensis* 'Rubra'), a hardy annual foliage plant.

◄ **Evening balm** The rich scent of white jasmine (*Jasminum officinale*) has been sweetening the summer evening air in British gardens since the 16th century. A vigorous climber, the jasmine is best grown up a sturdy, rustic trellis; here, its scrambling stems studded with clusters of white primrose-like flowers meet the silky seed heads of early-summer flowering *Clematis macropetala*. At their feet are neat clumps of purple-blue *Lavandula angustifolia* 'Hidcote'.

167

▲ **Ornamental herbs** Many aromatic herbs are decorative enough for the front of beds and borders. The scented, white-margined apple mint (*Mentha rotundifolia* 'Variegata') makes a good companion for the shining leaves of golden marjoram (*Origanum vulgare* 'Aureum').

▲ **Scented ground-cover** Aromatic purple-leaved sage makes an effective footing for spires of small-flowered butterfly gladiolus 'Melodie', with its salmon-pink blooms splashed with orange-scarlet. Flanking the late-summer gladioli are grass-like tufts of *Kniphofia* 'Maid of Orleans' topped by creamy-white flower spikes.

▶ **Sweet bergamot** Also known as Oswego tea and bee balm, sweet bergamot (*Monarda didyma*) is a hardy perennial whose scarlet flowers are beloved by bees and whose aromatic leaves can be dried and used in herbal teas. Its fiery colour is beautifully tempered by the silvery grey, felted foliage of cotton lavender (*Santolina chamaecyparissus*).

◀ **Miniature herb garden** A terracotta pot containing golden lemon balm (*Melissa officinalis* 'Aurea') is the aromatic centrepiece in a small herb bed that includes tarragon, purple-leaved sage and golden marjoram. Wild strawberries and sweet violets add their more delicate fragrances.

▲ **Pungent sage** The strongly flavoured common sage (*Salvia officinalis*) forms an attractive evergreen clump of narrow, grey-green leaves. There are several varieties with eye-catching coloured foliage which form a delightful mounded carpet when grown together. Here, grey-green sage is fronted by purple-leaved 'Purpurascens', white-variegated, purple-tinted 'Tricolor' and the gold-variegated 'Icterina'.

▶ **Ground-cover herbs** In sunny situations, low-growing herbs make effective weed-smothering ground-cover. Common marjoram (*Origanum vulgare*), a perennial culinary herb, bears aromatic leaves and large clusters of rose-pink flowers throughout summer. It makes a good companion for another excellent ground-cover plant, the purple-leaved bugle (*Ajuga reptans* 'Atropurpurea').

▼ **Mediterranean mood** A miniature southern hillside can be created from a collection of Mediterranean herbs. Here, in the background, aromatic, evergreen rosemary softens the pungent odour of blue-leaved rue (*Ruta graveolens* 'Jackman's Blue') and tempers the purple-leaved *Salvia officinalis* 'Purpurascens'. Silvery lamb's tongue (*Stachys lanata* 'Silver Carpet') and the pink flower heads of ornamental onion (*Allium karataviense*) make an attractive, low edging.

▲ **Flavoursome fennel** The most decorative of the culinary herbs, fennel (*Foeniculum vulgare*) is as much at home in the flower border as in the herb garden. It forms an airy bush, up to 1.8m (6ft) high, whose branching stems are clothed with aromatic foliage.
   The bronze-leaved form 'Purpureum' makes a stunning backdrop for groups of *Salvia haematodes*, whose tall stems bear lavender-blue flowers. In front, yellow-green lady's mantle (*Alchemilla mollis*) foams over the path.

scented stock (*Matthiola bicornis*) and sweet rocket (*Hesperis matronalis*) speak for themselves, as does that of evening primrose (*Oenothera biennis*).

Aromatic herbs

Garden herbs are often relegated to a corner of the vegetable plot, but many of these plants bear flowers or foliage which is much too attractive to be hidden away. They are splendid for associating not only with one another but also with other plants in the ornamental garden.

Few people have room for the traditional Elizabethan knot garden whose geometric contours were often edged with sweet-scented box or artemisias and filled with aromatic and medicinal herbs. But some of these classic partnerships can be re-created in small gardens: old-fashioned shrub roses with lavender or rosemary, fragrant thyme for ground-cover and pungent sage in patio pots.

The evergreen, blue-flowered rosemary will survive most

▼ **Scented nosegays** Dwarf varieties of tobacco plant (*Nicotiana alata*) are perfect for pots on the patio, where their delicious scent will linger through the summer months. 'Dwarf White Bedder', only 40cm (16in) high, remains open during the day.

▲ **Garden hyacinths** Perfectly hardy and available in colours ranging from white through shades of yellow, pink, red and orange to blue and purple, fragrant garden hyacinths should be planted in mass displays for maximum spring impact.

winters in Britain, provided it is given a sunny position, well-drained soil and adequate shelter from cold, drying winds. Its heady aroma scents the air on warm summer days, and small sprigs are marvellous additions to fresh and dried flower arrangements.

Chives (*Allium schoenoprasum*) are good scented edging plants for beds and borders, either on their own or mixed with variegated lemon-scented thyme (*Thymus × citriodorus* 'Silver Queen').

At the other end of the scale is the stately, aromatic angelica (*Angelica archangelica*) some 1.8m (6ft) tall. Its large leaves and domed flower heads look imposing against golden yews.

Other ornamental and fragrant herbs include the yellow-splashed ginger mint (*Mentha × gentilis* 'Variegata'), the golden lemon balm (*Melissa officinalis* 'Aurea') and sweet bergamot (*Monarda didyma* 'Croftway Pink').

As an added bonus, aromatic herbs can continue to scent the air indoors during winter. Many are ideal for drying and are traditional components of pot-pourri mixtures. Thyme, orange mint, rose geranium, lemon verbena, rosemary and sweet marjoram hold their fragrance well.

INDEX

Plants are listed under both the common name and the botanical name (which appears in italics). However, where both names are almost identical, page numbers follow the botanical name only.

ACKNOWLEDGEMENTS

Photographer's credits
Biofotos/Heather Angel 27, 51(b), 82, 97(t), 139, (Hazel le Rougetel) 71, 72(t), 74, 76(b); Michael Boys 70; Burda Magazines 151(tr); Ed Buziak 149; Brian Carter 60(br); Eric Crichton 4, 14(b), 17, 26, 30, 31(t), 40(b), 42(b), 45, 48(tr), 52(b), 53(t), 67(t), 75, 88, 89, 96, 102, 104, 106, 110, 111(b), 115(c), 118, 119, 120(t), 125, 133, 135, 136, 137, 138, 141, 144, 148(tl), 160, 161, 162(t), 164(bl), 165(c), 165(b), 166(t), 169(b), 172(b); Arnaud Descat 11, 22(t), 59(br), 84, 142; Philippe Ferret 92(t), 93(t), 107, 108(b), 112, 126, 134-35; Garden Picture Library 20(b), (Brian Carter) 34(t), 41, 91, 98(b), 152, 170, (Perdereau/Thomas) 12(t), 20(tl), 44, (David Russel) 128(t), (J Sira) 153, (R Sutherland) 10(t), 121(t), 150(tl), 151(br), 154, (D Willery) 169(b), (S Wooster) 94, 148(tr); John Glover 18(t), 28, 29(t),
33(br), 35(t), 80, 113, 162(b), 165(t); Derek Gould 50(c); Jerry Harpur 6, 69(b), 73(t), 109, 111(t), 129, 130, 143, 145, 157, (Magnus Ramsey) 127(b); Rob Herwig 51(t); Images Colour Library 164(br); Lamontagne 23(t), 33(t), 72(b), 92(bl), 92-3(b); Andrew Lawson 12(b), 16(tr), 36(t), 56, 59(t), 68, 98(t), 148(b); S & O Mathews front cover, 46(b), 65, 66(t), 114, 116, 121(b); Tania Midgley 1, 13. 14(t), 18(b), 52(t), 53(b), 66-67(b), 73(b), 79, 158-9; Natural Image (Bob Gibbons) 20(tr), 62(t), (R Fletcher) 34-35(b); Clive Nichols 3, 46(t), 47(tr), 47(b), 78, 99, 168; Perdereau/Thomas 25, 38, 39, 42(t), 43, 47(tl), 48(tl), 60(bl), 81, 83, 85, 86, 87, 105, 108(t), 140, 156, 172(t); Photos Horticultural 9, 19, 21, 22(b), 24, 29(b), 31(b), 32, 33(bl), 35(b), 36(b), 49, 50(t), 50(b), 51(c), 54, 57, 59(bl), 60(t), 93(br), 95, 97(b), 100, 117, 120(b), 122, 127(c), 128(b), 131, 132, 146, 147, 150(bl), 150-151; Harry Smith Collection 10(b), 16(tl), 34(bl), 58, 62(b), 64(t), 69(t), 90, 115(b), 163(t), 166(b), 167;
Jean-Paul Soulier 101; Elizabeth Whiting & Associates 40(t), (Karl-Dietrich Buhler) 8, 124.

Illustrators
Leonora Box 27, 40, 103, 104, 138(b); Wendy Bramell 64(b), 82; Lynn Chadwick 137; Colin Emberson 15(t), 28, 43; Sarah Fox-Davies 39, 48, 69, 163(t); Delyth Jones 10, 14, 16, 91; Nikki Kemball 11, 64(t), 79; Reader's Digest 17, 18, 19, 44, 55, 62, 66, 67, 68, 76, 80, 84, 88, 99, 106, 107, 110, 112, 134, 135, 136, 141, 144, 146, 167; Helen Senior 9, 63; Sally Smith 13, 45; Gill Tomblin 15(b), 56, 61, 94, 114, 126, 129, 132, 163(b), 164, 171; Barbara Walker 12, 25, 116, 130, 131; Ann Winterbotham 138(t).

Index compiled by Hilary Bird

Typesetting SX COMPOSING, ESSEX; Printing & Binding PRINTER INDUSTRIA, GRÁFICA S.A. BARCELONA
Separations COLOURSCAN OVERSEAS CO PTE LTD, SINGAPORE; Paper PERIGORD-CONDAT, FRANCE
53-009-2